PROJECT

MANAGER'S

HANDBOOK

—·—

WALKTHROUGH FOR BEGINNERS

VALENTYN BANNIKOV

CONTENTS

About the Author   IV

Dedication   VI

1. What is a project? What does a project   1
    manager responsible for?

2. Project, Program, Portfolio...   23

3. Initiation   46

4. Project Scope   68

5. Time Planning   90

6. Communication to Plan For   113

7. Risk Response   137

8. Progress Monitoring   160

9. Such an Important Closing Phase   182

ABOUT THE AUTHOR

Valentyn Bannikov is a certified (PMP, CSM, ICP-APM) technical Project & Program Management Professional equipped with a master's degree and 9+ years of success, building and guiding teams to execute large-scale client projects. Recognized for working across groups and leading project activities, including scope, planning, budgeting, staffing, KPI and milestones, stakeholder engagement, reporting, and delivery. Remarkable ability to foster and maintain strong relationships with teams, stakeholders, key decision-makers, and vendors to drive innovation, improvement, and scalability of global organizations. Primary areas of expertise include the following:

- Project management and leadership

- Complete project lifecycle experience

- Agile, waterfall and hybrid application development

- Business process analysis and improvement

- Risk management

- Release management

This book is dedicated to the pillars of my life, my family who influenced me throughout my life and shaped me to become a better person.

This book is dedicated to my younger self and my mentees.

This book is dedicated to all Ukrainians fighting for their freedom and independece.

CHAPTER 1

WHAT IS A PROJECT? WHAT DOES A PROJECT MANAGER RESPONSIBLE FOR?

Project management, as opposed to traditional management, is considered one of the most effective ways to develop a business, and this model works successfully for personal goals as well. To master the art of project management, you need to understand the basic terms and mechanics of the whole process, which is what this book is about.

What Is a Project?

Let's start our discussion of the topic by defining what constitutes a project and what does not.

The term "project" comes from the Latin word *projectus*, which literally means "thrown forward". Nowadays, the meaning of the word has more of a metaphorical content – we "throw forward" an idea to make it a reality. The word "project" in the theory of project management is commonly understood as a set of actions, limited in time, aimed at the development of a new product with given parameters.

The main criteria for a project are considered to be its features as follows:

- a definite delivery time,

- a clear goal,

- limited resources,

- unique goals or ways of achieving the goal.

A project focused on resolving a singular issue is referred to as a **monoproject**. When multiple monoprojects are combined, a **multiproject** is formed, leading to the creation of a single product. Several multiprojects can then be combined to form a **megaproject**, which is managed and funded centrally. Megaprojects are characterized by their large scale, implementation within national and regional boundaries, and cost starting at one billion dollars and upwards.

Megaprojects are often not only economically or socially significant, but also politically. A country that implements them claims a strong economy and unlimited resources, forcing its partners and opponents to reckon with its interests. For example, the construction of the aircraft Antonov AN-225 Mriya, showed the level of development of aircraft construction.

Other megaprojects include the Manhattan atomic bomb program, the Channel Tunnel, the Panama Canal expansion, the Large Hadron Collider, the Vostok space program, the Port Mann Bridge construction in Vancouver, and a COVID-19 vaccine. The list does not end there, of course.

However, not all significant acts in human history can be called megaprojects, as on closer examination they do not belong to the concept of "project" as a whole.

The theory of project management states that projects cannot include operational and functional activities, such as work on an assembly line or the routine performance of duties – business correspondence, document management, and machinery upgrades. The project shall be unique, often a breakthrough in some direction.

Project initiators, in fact, can not be 100% sure (but have the right to dream and believe) that their vision is bound to succeed, because they are creating something that has never been done before.

It is often enough to hear that our whole life is one megaproject broken up into thousands of projects. In common life this is true, but in terms of project management it is not so simple and poetic. Our life is more of a routine, as biologically our bodies are in a state of homeostasis, i.e. they are busy maintaining their own constant state. The same can be applied to our domestic problems because most of life is taken up with daily chores. A project could probably be called getting an education, having a child or moving house, but up to a certain point.

In other words, a project can be described as a time- and resource-limited undertaking that results in a unique goal or uses unique ways of achieving it.

What Is Project Management?

The project manager, or PM, is a key person in project management. His role can be described in two main phrases: he is responsible for the project to fit within the project triangle, which we will describe below, as well as he is responsible for the whole project.

The PM is the key person in the whole project, the team leader, since he or she is responsible for the actions of the many specialists to end in the same planned result.

According to the tasks, the manager sets the goal for which the project is being developed. The goal should be based on a customer's wishes, but it should be formulated in a way that is professional and understandable to the implementer.

The goal dictates the construction of the project concept, i.e. it formulates the main project task and defines its achievement methods. The project concept should be clear to the team and to the customer.

By the time the project takes on its original shape and form, which can change as the project evolves, the project manager begins to work on the budget, coordinating it with the customer at each stage.

Once you have a concept and a budget, you can start to build a team, if it is not permanent, and assign roles to it at each project stage. It is important to qualify applicants in time, selecting specialists whose competencies match the project tasks.

From this point, the manager starts to work directly on the project which consists in discussing specific details with experts in the relevant field. A full understanding of all the nuances is achieved, the team begins to interact constructively, and the strategy and tactics for the project and the scope for each stage are scheduled.

Based on the conceptual plan, the PM should develop terms of reference for each team member and communicate them to the implementers. If they have any questions, now is the time to answer them and avoid misunderstandings.

During project implementation, the project manager coordinates the activities of the experts, supervises their actions, and monitors the deadlines for each scheduled stage. The PM is also responsible for communicating with the customer before, during and after the project, so he or she should discuss the project implementation step by step. When the project is completed, the project manager presents the result. If the customer has no complaints and is happy with the result – the project is completed, if not, it is necessary to discuss the reason for dissatisfaction, fix what needs fixing, or convince the customer that he is wrong.

Clearly, this is a general list of tasks, and each real project requires an individual approach and flexibility from the manager.

The project manager has one of the main tools of project management in his hands – a **project management triangle**. It is also called an iron triangle, but the sense is that this geometric figure is impermanent and quite mobile, which is not very consistent with the qualities that the word "iron" implies.

The term "project management triangle" visualizes the basic complexity of any project – the latter is constrained by three main factors: cost, time, and the scope of work to be done during the project. Perhaps these three sides of the triangle would not be so important if the project work was not associated with a key concept such as the original product quality.

The triangle shows the relationship and mutual influence of its edges, i.e. the scope of planned work, financial and time constraints. The relationship lies in the fact that it is impossible to change the length of one edge without affecting the other, or even both remaining sides of the triangle.

Let's take for example a project of building a skyscraper with a height of N floors in a given time and with a budget of N dollars. So we have a beautiful equilateral project management triangle, and with these parameters, the project guarantees an excellent result. And now the trench has been dug, contractors hired, heavy construction equipment rented for the right dates. The project manager is satisfied: the deadline is met and there is every chance for a magnificent completion of the project. At that very moment, the customer shows up and tells him that he needs the skyscraper not in a certain time frame, but much earlier, which shifts one of the triangle bases, turning the project from a firmly grounded object into the Leaning Tower of Pisa. The thing is that the reduction of construction time is possible only if the customer agrees either to a skyscraper with fewer amount floors, or to increase the budget. It is impossible to build N floors in the new time frame, as you will have to hire more workers, more equipment, pay for urgent delivery of materials, etc.

Despite the fact that the project management triangle has no additional "spare" edges, there is another parameter of project success, which can be fitted inside this figure. It is about customer satisfaction with the product they received as a result of the project. If the project fits within the project management triangle, and the customer is satisfied with the result, the project can be considered successful.

The project manager not only performs all assigned tasks but is also **responsible for the project**. Unfortunately, no one is immune from failures, so the project can fail at any stage, and then the responsibility will be on PM only. The customer won't take any excuses. It doesn't matter who is to blame – contractors or circumstances, the manager cannot blame any third-party events, he will still be to blame for what happened.

The only way not to be a scapegoat is obvious to anyone who has dealt with project management. The manager should detect weak spots in his team in advance, as well as consider all possible risks. When forming a project, the PM should draw up terms of reference for himself, providing for possible pitfalls that will surely appear all of a sudden. Murphy's law, which says, that if anything that can go wrong will go wrong, works just fine.

***

Evaluating the Manager's Authority

If a project manager is invested in such responsibility, he should also have broad powers to stimulate the team. For example, he should have the power to replace a professional who fails to perform his or her duties, impose penalties for rule-breakers, and have the ability to reward employees who demonstrate a high level of professionalism and set a good example for others.

An understanding of the type of organization in which the PM works can help in this regard. They can be functional, project, matrix and flat.

Functional organizations have a classic management hierarchy and employees work in departments, organized according to a professional basis. These are usually production organizations. The project manager in such an organization will have to work with all the heads of departments and divisions, as well as the directorate, which will complicate his task and narrow his authority.

A **project organization** implies a type of management set up specifically for project work of up to two years duration. The work is entirely project-oriented, so in this structure the PM will have every opportunity to influence his subordinates.

A **matrix organization** structure combines functional and project types. If the organization is more oriented towards the functional type, it is a simplified, or weak, matrix structure. A strong matrix structure is closer to a project structure. A third type of matrix structure is a balanced one, combining both functional and project types in equal proportions. The manager builds his team for the project life, and during this period his authority is broad enough to control the implementation of the tasks.

A **flat structure** is a type of management organization with no middle management. It is characterized by high accountability of subordinates and rapid management response to difficulties, so a flat structure is conducive to the work of the project manager.

―――ぬ―――

Project Life Cycle

Projects have their own life cycles, which we will discuss in more detail in the following chapters of the book, but a general idea should be given in advance.

The first stage is **initiation**. At the very beginning of a project, when there is a lot of discussion and the goal formation and ways of implementation start. At this stage, the project charter is formulated, as well as the main points and agreements, which become the basic project documents.

Planning is the stage when a project roadmap is formed. A team is assigned, roles, resources, and a budget are allocated, and a schedule of upcoming work is drawn up.

At the project startup stage, the manager focuses on "starting" the project work mechanism, monitoring personnel activities at the initial stage, finding and eliminating mistakes.

Monitoring is the most important stage because it allows for adjustments in the workflow. The manager should check how accurately the company is meeting its goals, and whether there are any underestimated difficulties or unexpected problems.

And finally comes the project **closing**. The manager reports back to the customer and signs the completion documents with him. At this stage, it is especially important to correct mistakes, because the memories of project activities are very fresh in mind.

Projects go through the same stages but differ in type, which should be taken into account before starting work on the project.

The first project type is **predictive** when in the first phase (initiation) the manager already knows what means, terms and scope of work will restrain him in the future.

For example – projects that develop stage by stage, are also called "waterfall". The disadvantage of this type is that if at the initial stage an error was made, then later it will be almost impossible to correct.

The **iterative** project type appeared to refine the previous type, for which iterations were introduced – a series of repetitive cycles. Each iteration includes planning, development, testing, and analysis. This task is assigned to cross-functional teams, interacting with others and being responsible for the result as much as the others. The model allows for necessary changes to be made to the project and for better results to be achieved.

The **incremental** life cycle was created to speed up processes and get the product out in much less time. To do this, a minimum viable product was already created in the first iterations and improved in the remaining iterations. Thus, the customer could get the result in the course of the project, before the final refinement, and could see the result of the money invested.

An even more progressive model is the **adaptive** project life cycle, combining the advantages of the previous two models – iterative and incremental. Through iterations, taking from a couple of weeks to a month, necessary adjustments are constantly being made to the project, which improves the product quality. Iteration combines several processes, with the former involving planning. Regular interaction between the team and the customer allows the tasks to be solved at the required level.

To draw an analogy, the project life cycle can be compared to a chess game, consisting of three stages: the opening, i.e. the project initiation, the middle game (monitoring & controlling), and the endgame, which is the project closure. Between initiation and closure, there is a major chess battle with attack, defense, and its combination or, when viewed from the project perspective, the Deming cycle, consisting of planning, implementation, monitoring and controlling.

The Deming cycle is worth mentioning in more detail. In the 1950s, economist William Deming became interested in the work of engineer Walter Shewhart on the problem of product quality management. Shewhart proposed that the sequence "plan-do-check" should be carried out in cycles, and Deming added the stage of product defect correction and elimination.

The model is also referred to as PDCA\PDSA, which is an acronym for: Plan – Do – Check\Study – Act.

Thanks to the Deming cycle, you can optimize and improve your project work.

The product quality, created as the project result, will be high if you work using a phase gate concept. A project consists of several phases, elements of the project life cycle that are logically linked, with each phase culminating in a specific achievement. To move on to the next phase, it is necessary to make sure that the completed part of the work "passes through the gate", i.e. is performed in compliance with the quality criteria. If the phase does not meet established quality parameters, it is necessary to return to it and make the required corrections. An undetected and uncorrected mistake will manifest itself in subsequent phases, which is why it is important to check the product throughout the project phase by phase.

Imagine a hypothetical situation: you have built that N-story skyscraper, but forgot about the elevator! Now you can't add it to the project, that is, attach it to the building in some way...

It is essential to keep in mind that the cost of mistakes at the project start is close to zero, they can be corrected quickly, but the closer we get to the end of the project, the more expensive it can be.

So, now you know certain key concepts of project management, and we can go further down the road of knowledge.

CHAPTER 2

— • —

PROJECT, PROGRAM, PORTFOLIO...

Bound By One Goal

We have already discussed the concept of a project and what can and cannot be considered a project in the first chapter of this book, but now we will discuss the project portfolio and program within the project management context. As you begin or continue your PM career, you will come across these concepts more than once, as they are a vital part of what we do.

So, whichever sector of the economy an organization belongs to, its activities are organisationally divided into two main types: process and project. The main difference is that a process is cyclical, while a project is unique and time-bound and is created to achieve a goal within a specific time frame with predetermined resources.

In this book, we will mainly discuss the implementation of different projects – from their initiation to their closure, but project management is not limited to this. It teaches how to work not only with the project itself from the inside but also takes us beyond it, expanding the scope of PM's activities.

Each project, while unique, can be part of a common cause, and its goal and product can only be part of a wider goal and global product. In this case, we mean project programs or portfolios.

Some organizations set up several projects simultaneously, each generating a small income. By combining them into a single program, business management achieves better results, including in terms of profit, than by working with each project individually. The program includes a centralized allocation of resources – financial, human, and other, as well as well-crafted timing and other effective ways to manage. Thus, working on projects by combining them into a program is the best way to achieve your goal.

How long does a program last? Considering that every project is finite, the program lasts as long as the longest project is included, and not longer.

Thus, the concept of a program in project management can be defined as follows: it is the unification of several projects, aimed at achieving the same goal, into one group to provide the most effective management.

ele

Program Manager's Tasks

Project management provides that each project, program, and one step ahead, each portfolio, has its own manager. In each case and at each level, the manager's tasks are defined according to project, program or portfolio features and goals, and we will discuss them in more detail.

Let's start with the program manager's tasks. He regulates the movement of activities between projects in the accountable group and access to resources and makes sure that performers do not stray from the course taken. It is his duty to communicate with project managers, keep up to speed, and understand interrelationships between fellow project managers.

Planning, developed by the program manager covers a set of projects that comprise it. He develops a general schedule to coordinate the work of all projects, and his risk response also applies to the program as a whole. The manager's work at this level can be defined as supervisory because he is focused on leading multiple projects toward a single goal.

The program manager does not have to monitor all stages – from the start-up to the final stage – in the project development in this group. He should only be aware of what is happening basically, but should not be interested in the details. If the program manager feels that one of the projects becomes problematic, complicating the program management, he should act according to the rules, developed for this case for his position.

From the start of the program to the end, the manager should concentrate as much as possible on identifying the benefits to develop the case and then analyze them to select the most effective and promising opportunities. Having these data available, the program manager ensures that the benefits he or she considers necessary are achieved in the short term. At the same time, if he feels that a certain project does not meet certain tasks, he gets onto it: if he can correct some positions, he does so, and those projects that are deemed ineffective are excluded from the program.

One of the most important manager's tasks is to control the interrelation of projects. He decides which project should be a priority at the moment, and which products of other projects will form the basis for subsequent projects. The program manager develops a roadmap for how the program will approach the goal. While working on the most promising ideas for an entire group of projects, the program manager should not forget that one of his most important tasks is the organizational changes required to achieve the goal. When he or she makes decisions about program projects, his or her task is to keep his or her colleagues informed of the changes.

Project Portfolio – Basic Concept

The project portfolio is a collection of projects, programs and other work that is grouped together to facilitate the effective management of that work to meet strategic business objectives. The projects or programs of the portfolio may not necessarily be interdependent or directly related.

A portfolio is created to achieve strategic goals and is managed by an individual with specific responsibilities. It is difficult to be sure how many project and program portfolios an organization can have; it all depends on how many activities it runs. The most essential thing is to decide which projects should be included in the portfolio and which are better left for the future. The need to save money often results in a very critical view of the quality and cost of projects, which is a good thing because it forces management to stimulate teams to focus on the best solutions. Thus, the product quality goes up and the price of the product goes down.

The basic question that a manager has to address is as follows: "How effective and economical are our projects?"

When mentioning project programs, most of the time we imply one organization's activities. Competitors' projects, which, each from their own side, are trying to get the same benefit, cannot be put together in the same portfolio.

But not all of the projects of the same company are put together in the same portfolio, only those that meet the same goal. It is clear that the main goal of any commercial enterprise is to make a profit, all company projects are aimed at that in one way or another, but we have to narrow down the goals to an acceptable value to simplify the project portfolio formation. Otherwise, the task portfolio will be unsustainable. In other words, there will be as many project portfolios as the company has set for itself. Let's take an example.

Let's say we build houses. We have a portfolio for office buildings, a portfolio for cottages, and a portfolio for industrial buildings. Let's say we get an order for a multi-storey public car park, and we realize that we are ready to work with such projects in the future, so we form a new portfolio – for car parks.

Or, for example, you and I decide to increase productivity in the company, and we do it in a number of different ways. In consultation with the team, we decide to improve discipline by developing a system of penalties for lateness and failure to comply with duties, training specialists, hiring a psychologist, arranging a canteen for employees, etc. For each of these tasks, we initiate a separate project and put them all into one portfolio.

A project portfolio is convenient.

- By grouping projects according to goals, we will be able to control their performance, taking into account the combination of activities undertaken to implement each of them.

- The portfolio makes it possible to calculate the budget to achieve a specific goal and control costs, understanding how much is spent on this direction.

- Working with projects, distributed by target area, facilitates monitoring and analysis of activities. Finally, the head of the company receives much more relevant data to estimate the success of the company as a whole.

- Using portfolios, we get more data to properly prioritize, and we also make risk management much easier.

- The project portfolio allows for more flexibility in terms of resources. For example, it is possible to allocate a specially trained department of experts who work only on projects from a specific portfolio. Specialization in a particular area will allow them to achieve better results and improve the quality of their activities.

- Management of multiple projects becomes a manageable task, and this applies to projects from the same portfolio as well as from different ones.

- Using a portfolio, managers can abandon a project if it is no longer fit for purpose.

In large companies, you can't do without project portfolios at all! It is much easier to select the most cost-effective ones by relating projects to each other, and if a manager sees a pile of papers with different ideas, sooner or later he or she will simply get tired of "digesting" them. Portfolios make it possible to evaluate projects systematically and adequately.

In many companies, as is evident in practice, project selection becomes a cause for misunderstanding and sometimes conflict. Project portfolios allow you to reduce negative situations and address the issue of selection intelligently, based on objective comparative data. By the way, the decision-making period is reduced, because stakeholders have the maximum amount of information.

Practice shows that implementation of the project portfolio system increases the company's efficiency in achieving its goals. Apparently, the whole point is that the portfolio dictates an organized approach to project activities, and order is always better than chaos. It all seems simple and understandable, but the trouble is that we know so many great ways to succeed, and somehow each time we find even more reasons not to use them.

Experience in this area is just as significant. If you already know how to manage a project, it's time to go further – to work with project portfolios. It calls for mastering the art of project management.

Portfolio Manager's Responsibilities

A portfolio manager's main job is to manage a project portfolio. Project Portfolio Management (PPM), is the next stage in a project manager's career, higher and more interesting. Mastering this skill without knowing how to manage a project is quite challenging. You should understand the very essence of project activities, and know a variety of nuances that can be learned and mastered only in the work on the project. In short, PPM is a task for the trained!

The most essential thing, in this case, is to understand which project is most likely to lead to the set goal or come close to its achievement. The main mission of a manager responsible for the implementation of projects combined in a single portfolio is to manage all portfolios in an organized manner to achieve the goals set. Like the program manager, he should see the task as a whole, in its entirety. Based on his tasks, he should understand how the result will be achieved, how and when the projects will be implemented, and their sequence and conditions.

A portfolio manager is a person able to see the tasks as a whole and in the context of the main goals of the organization. Can you develop the intuition to instantly determine whether a project is worth spending time and money on? Absolutely! It is a matter of experience, and when you have accumulated enough of it, the quantity will turn into quality.

The project system itself is not simple, and when you start learning how to manage a project portfolio, at first you will feel like you are stepping on thin, slippery ice. Indeed, project management is a tactic, but managing a group of projects is a strategy that requires serious work and thinking globally.

Nowadays, organizations and businesses cannot take on as many projects as they would like, resources are usually limited, time is short and external circumstances can compromise plans. The management team, therefore, develops certain strategies based on benefits and logic to select those projects and programs that will fit into the portfolio and whose implementation will help achieve the goal in the most cost-effective and fastest way possible. The strategy should also include tools for sequencing the projects and programs and making up the portfolio.

You need to prioritize, reasonably assess the project idea, and be able to predict whether the product will be up to your expectations.

The best tactic is to focus on the concept of a project's potential return, which will be key to its acceptance. Sometimes it is necessary to weigh analyze the data of several sites, and they may be identical, in which case you should give preference to the project whose potential return is higher.

When selecting new projects, the manager, responsible for the entire portfolio should not forget about the evaluation of implemented ideas. Once the project is implemented and closed, the manager should ask for and review the closing date. First and foremost, he should assess the ROI and then everything else.

—⁓—

Fundamentals of PPM Management

Project portfolio management involves balancing projects by taking into account their risks, duration, and other parameters. A well-formed portfolio will enable the team to achieve its goals. Portfolio balance is ensured by the organization's activities to work out or search for new projects, to develop opportunities opening up in the market. By replenishing the portfolio with the most promising ones, the manager achieves the stability of the portfolio contents, not allowing possible (and unavoidable) risks to disturb the positive forecast achieved. In all circumstances, the project portfolio riskiness should not be so high as to lose everything in the same time period.

Project management is also used to assess risks in advance and to try to shape the portfolio so that high-risk projects make up a minor portion. Risks can derail all efforts; they need to be controlled as early as the portfolio coordination stage.

Project grouping is not a one-off task, but the work of several months, sometimes even years, if we mean global state and interstate megaprojects consisting of multiple project portfolios. Suppose a country with an underdeveloped economy decides to organize an industry that will bring the country's standard of living up to an average level compared to neighboring countries. This project would include mining, processing industry construction, machine tool industry, auto industry, building new roads, etc. The plans alone will take several years to develop. But how not to get it wrong, how to choose the projects that are most needed for the main task? The best method is monitoring and control. The portfolio manager should constantly check and analyze what is going on while concluding the portfolio contents.

You should be prepared for one or more projects to be dropped from the group, as they no longer meet the organization's tasks. After monitoring and analysis, the project prioritization may change, as well as their sequence.

The same work is done on the total duration of the project portfolio. It is necessary to correctly calculate which timelines will be optimal to achieve the goals, and projects with a duration exceeding the obtained data will have to be postponed.

Project management moves along a vector from top to bottom, that is, the projects that are at the top of the list, as the most low-risk and potentially the most effective, go to work first. They are provided with the necessary resources and do not skimp on their implementation. Those projects in the lower positions get their chance only after the priorities are implemented. In this way, resources do not flow through the fingers and do not disperse throughout the portfolio, so they are difficult to even trace afterward, let alone collect again. Resource planning adds value to the business.

The portfolio manager should act as a diplomat toward all his colleagues who manage projects directly. Each of them wants to push their own agenda, then get some bonuses from the company during the budgeting phase or implementation, but the portfolio manager cannot forget about their interests by underestimating the value of the work. The portfolio manager establishes communication, reduces the intensity of disagreements, translates them into a substantive conversation, and achieves transparency in the relationship.

— *ele* —

Project – Program – Portfolio. What Are the Differences?

The project manager's areas of responsibility, the program manager, and the portfolio manager are distinct and complementary. None of these positions can be eliminated without loss, because each of the management team, usually mid-level executives, is uniquely empowered.

Project managers are each responsible for their own area of work and oversee the phases from start to finish. Their level is the first and most important in its own way, because they create the real end product, while program and portfolio managers operate with concepts detached from reality, essentially abstractions. If project managers fail to fulfill their duties, the entire hierarchical pyramid will collapse, and the detailed plans and high-minded strategies of senior managers will remain mere words. Being aware of the level of his work significance, a project manager often has to remind his superiors of his task value. He can remind them of the resources required and assert the designated level of his project priority.

The most important thing about a project manager's work is the day-to-day management, routine, precisely measured, and specified actions in the project's charter.

The program manager, as mentioned above, no longer gets into project implementation and its needs. The program manager coordinates the implementation of several projects, adjusts the goal accuracy, integrates activity results, and makes the system work efficiently, effectively, and according to target goals.

The program manager works for the tactical coordination of all parties involved in the projects in his program.

The description of a portfolio manager's responsibilities is not much different from that of a program manager, the most important distinction being the level, at which portfolio managers work. They are entrusted to lead the ship to the far shore, so they look farthest and see more than anyone else. Their job is not to lose their bearings or lead the ship in the opposite direction.

The portfolio manager is responsible for a comprehensive strategic initiative. Only they can fully answer the question "Why?" as they know the ultimate goal of the entire organization.

How do managers in such different positions work together and not conflict? Mutual understanding depends on how well colleagues understand each other's work; how ready they are to work together toward a common goal. The company management has to maintain a policy of mutual cooperation, respect, and desire to help, and find a way out of a difficult situation through discussion and dialogue.

Projects are part of a program; a program and a project are parts of a portfolio; they can only be successfully implemented if managers control them as a whole.

Chapter 3

---·---

Initiation

Where Do Projects Start?

I n the previous chapter, we listed the basic stages of a project, the first of which is initiation. Now we are going to expand that definition.

According to the PMI PMBoK standard, developed by the Project Management Institute – PMI (USA), initiation in the context of project management is a series of processes formed into a group of activities. They are used to assess prospects of the future project idea, as well as prepare and launch the project implementation.

The stage begins before the project, which allows you to review in advance possible strategies for goal achievement, and sometimes the goal itself. If it is done responsibly and thoughtfully, the project manager will be able to anticipate any risks and make the ground for the future. Subsequently, the people in charge of the project will no longer be able to operate with such a wide range of possibilities for adjustment, because they will be limited by the project framework, including interrelated triangle parameters: finances – terms – scope of work.

The initiation phase determines if the idea is deserving of the resources required to make it a reality. Gradually, as the essence of the project crystallizes, the manager prepares the main documents for upcoming activities: a business case, a project charter, and an assumption log. Once the key participants in the project have signed these documents, the project is considered to have started, and then the second stage, planning, comes in, but we will discuss it in the next chapter.

Who the Sponsor Is And Who They Can Be

Despite the importance of the manager's role, he or she is not the only person in charge of the project. Depending on the project scope and other conditions, there are other people who work with him and on whom the success of the undertaking depends. In addition to the team, they are a customer and a sponsor or supervisor.

The customer is more or less self-explanatory: it is a person, group of people, or state organization which will be able to use the resulting product in the future. The role of the sponsor, on the other hand, is not so straightforward.

In the average person's mind, a sponsor is someone who gives money. But in project management, it is somewhat different. A sponsor subsidizes resources in a broader sense because a successful project sometimes requires the support of authorities, the loyalty of public opinion, or perhaps connections in scientific, business or political circles. The sponsor is more of a "magic wand"' for the project.

In the project management context, a sponsor is a person responsible for the project, just like the manager, but his position is outside the project and his scope is outside the triangle because the sponsor's authority is wider and his position and status are noticeably higher than that of the manager. A sponsor is often called the project supporter, which is justified since it is usually a person holding high positions in the company implementing the project itself or even in power structures. This is the person the manager comes to when faced with a very difficult problem.

For example, at the last moment, the city administration refuses to sign necessary documents, and bureaucratic turmoil ensues. The manager, who has no time to run to the officials, approaches the sponsor, who finds legitimate ways to change the situation.

It goes without saying that the supervisor, or sponsor, has as much interest in the project as anyone else involved. His interest may be financial, but sometimes it is based on a different motivation. For example, the supervisor needs the credit of public recognition, which will go to him if the project is implemented successfully.

The supervisor's tasks during the project implementation are wide-ranging. They include expenditure monitoring of funds, participating in the business plan development, approving the main project documents, and cooperating with the manager. Besides, the supervisor has considerable powers. For example, he can appoint

or remove the manager from his position.
His position outside the triangle allows him
to monitor developments in the surrounding
economic, social or political environment and
adjust strategy and tactics to achieve his goals.

At the initiation stage, the sponsor performs a
key task. If he or she is a contracting organization
employee, he or she correlates the project
goal with the whole organization's goal. The
supervisor signs the project's main documents
and participates in discussions with applicants for
the manager's position. As mentioned above, his
or her area of management includes resources,
both financial and professional, as well as business
and personal communication channels, which are
particularly important at the project start.

The supervisor can share his experience if it is
needed by the team or the project manager, he
should always be aware of what is going on,
celebrate successes, and draw attention to failures

for analysis. He or she can act as an arbitrator in team conflicts, for which he or she should have veto power.

In the previous chapter we discussed the manager's responsibility and the sponsor's presence in the project does not change anything. Compared to the supervisor, the manager is the main person in charge of the project, he keeps up to the project's speed, and if something goes wrong, he reports it to the supervisor.

If you compare a sponsor with a customer, the difference is that the latter doesn't have to get into the team's or manager's problems, he just sets a task and demands its timely implementation in a quality manner. In the project management history, there have been cases when the sponsor and the customer have been the same person, but this is the exception rather than the rule. The customer can contribute to the project with the means available to him, but he will not be approached for support in case of problems. Moreover, the customer will try not to get involved in the details if the project unexpectedly finds itself in a problematic situation. There is a sponsor for this, who has the necessary leverage. In the end, the sponsor reports to the customer, not the other way around.

As the simplest example, you can take the construction of a country house. Let's say you bought the land and ordered the architect to do a project with support services. In this case, you are the customer, if only because you pay all the costs. The architect hires a crew of builders to whom he is ready to entrust the project implementation, and the work begins. Now the architect becomes the supervisor, or sponsor, and the master builder becomes the project manager. The architect is interested in the result, he controls the crew's work, interacts with the customer, attracts resources, and hires the right specialists. This is the sponsor's role in project management.

The chain is lined up.

So you visit a construction site and you don't like something there. You have the right to tell your ideas to the foreman and even get him to redo the work to your liking, but your interference can put a brake on the plan, and instead of a house you get a monument to your stupidity. Therefore, all claims are reasonable to discuss with the supervisor, and he will decide what to do.

_____ ℓℓ _____

Let's define the triangle

Let me remind you: the initiation is the debut stage, so the manager is not yet limited to three edges of the project triangle, meaning there is no responsibility for the implementation of activities yet either. And until the business case and the project charter have been drawn up, it is premature to hold him or her accountable for the project's progress.

If you are to act as a manager, remember: it's a sink-or-swim world. During this period, the manager can and should fix the lack of a framework without getting entangled in a vague and unspecified, and essentially non-existent, plan. You wouldn't sit down to play chess or cards without knowing the rules of the game, would you?

In the debut phase, when the project idea is still under discussion, only a rough estimate (ROM estimate) of the upcoming time and financial costs is possible. The same is right for the work scope. Sponsors, customers and all stakeholders will be eager to get exact figures from the manager and will get tired of hearing: "Will it be finished by January? And by February?", as well as: "Are we going to stay within 40 million...? Are you sure?" It is important to point out to everyone who is curious that the estimates you give at the project initiation stage are approximate, and can have a wide range of variations. Your job as a manager is to get very approximate figures accepted, taking into account multiple amendments to come.

Let's go back to a rough estimate concept, as it is very significant. ROM is an abbreviation of "A Rough Order of Magnitude". The ROM estimate determines crucial things such as the project strategy and the whole planning phase following the initiation.

The rough estimate is necessary as it forms the basis for the upcoming budget and decides whether it is feasible and whether it is worth going into a project with such a financial framework. The ROM tool is often used by companies to select projects that can be implemented and determine the order of projects if there is more than one.

The ROM is used until the customer or initiator can get down to business and determine the exact cost, time and other resources to be spent. Despite the uncertainties, envisaged when generating data based on the application of rough estimation, this data remains in operation for the duration of the project.

With ROM data, the manager can forecast the upcoming project work, so he or she needs to be involved in a triangle formation. Sometimes it does not work, as the manager comes into the project after the basic documents have been completed, and then he or she finds himself or herself in a "go there, don't know where" situation. Even worse for the forthcoming project is the relationship when the project manager is at beck and call of the customer, sponsor and other high-ranking people. The triangle is likely to be stacked behind his back, and if the manager tries to argue that the project scope is not consistent with the ROM figures, he will not be listened to.

The manager will then not be well supported, and if (or when) the project fails, he or she will be the one who gets the brunt of it.

On this basis, at the initiation stage it is important for the manager, in addition to all the tasks of the stage itself, to take the right position in the project executing structure between the team, the customer and the supervisor, and to build business relationships with all participants in the forthcoming project, regardless of the official hierarchy.

Business case and project charter

The project business case is a starting point; it reflects the final product idea. Before you start to formulate this crucial document, you need to understand its importance in project management.

This document is rarely prepared for small-scale projects, unless it is to participate in an initiative competition and needs to show its worth.

The business case content should reflect all the arguments that developers of the new idea can offer in order to prove the upcoming project's necessity. The business case should be a compilation of all possible competitive considerations, and it should be presented in such a way that any objections are brushed aside in the bud. However, the business case should contain comprehensive information, even if there is some data that may raise further questions.

The business case needs to be written in a way that will interest the right person who will sponsor the project and provide the right perspective. For example, sometimes it is necessary to present secondary results that are not directly related to the project goal. The main thing is to give a prospective sponsor the feeling that this particular idea meets all his wishes. If the business case is well prepared, the sponsor will be found and become the engine of the project.

The business case should give a full, clear, structured presentation of the project for decision-makers to accept or reject the project and see all its advantages compared to other similar ideas. The project budget and economics should not be left out, because data on forthcoming costs will be assessed in a particularly picky manner. As the manager still only has a rough estimate, this data will not give a detailed picture of all the costs to be incurred, but at this stage nothing else can be proposed.

The business case structure depends on the project itself, on the purposes for which the document is created, and many other circumstances. It is usually structured according to certain standards.

First, it is necessary to present the initial conditions, preferably critical and dire, analyzing which it is clear that the implementation of this project will be the only way for the situation to be resolved in a favorable way. This part is traditionally called the background, or prerequisites.

The second part of the business case should outline how this very project, presented here and now, can solve the problems of the day and make the world a better place. The project description should sound positive and look literally like a panacea.

Then it is worth outlining the changes to occur after the problem is solved and the benefits that will accrue to the people who participated in the project implementation. It may motivate the likely sponsor and others who make the decision on the project.

It is desirable for the business shall offer a choice among several strategy options, which always forces you to think about the proposal and get into it for at least a certain period of time.

Finally, it is possible to mention some specific disadvantages that will occur during the project implementation or will manifest themselves after the project closing and product delivery.

Once the business case has helped to achieve the desired result and the project has been approved, it is time to start working with the next most important document – the project charter, which defines the rules of the game, without which a winner cannot be identified.

The project charter is to be taken seriously. It should be the very basic document, reflecting the project's unchangeable data. What will not change from the start of the project until the product is delivered. If the business case was needed at a certain point and to achieve a certain goal, the charter should be formed with the future of the whole project in mind.

Sometimes, it is necessary to provide several revisions of the charter to reflect the main project goals in a correct and accurate manner.

The charter structure is simple. The main part of this document should contain the project's full name with a short description and the start date. In the same part, data of the sponsor and the project manager, and other stakeholders.

The charter states how the project is related to the main strategic line of the whole company if projects are implemented within a particular company. The charter should formulate basic requirements to be met by actions of the team implementing the project, as well as the tasks to be achieved by the participants during the project implementation.

It is hard to overestimate the importance of the charter. This document formulates the main phase gates of a project, and gives a product definition. It allows all participants to propose their ideas about the project to reach a common agreement. The charter lays out the ground rules by which the team will work, it brings everyone involved in the project together, and helps delineate areas of responsibility.

Assumption Log

Before the project starts, neither the supervisor, manager nor team members know how things will go and what conditions they will have to work under. Nevertheless, they can anticipate different developments in the future. It is impossible to guarantee that life will follow the plan, so expectations of project participants will be entered into the Assumption Log.

Low-level assumptions are entered into the log for simple operations, while high-level assumptions, such as strategy, are reflected in the business case. With the assumptions, the project manager will be able to assess risks in advance and manage them.

Work on this document starts at the initiation phase in parallel with the work on the business case. Given the importance of completing the assumption log, it is essential that this document is endorsed by the customer and the sponsor.

***

Project manager's mistakes at the initiation phase

Given the importance of this stage, the manager should avoid typical mistakes.

First, PM should not be an "egoist" who thinks that he or she alone can use the ROM correctly, draft the business case and charter, and calculate and anticipate all possible assumptions.

When one becomes a project manager, one remains a mere human being, not plugged into the world's intelligence. If he intends to do his job properly at the initiation stage, he should delegate some authority to experts in the field of evaluation, and himself, having modestly studied their work results, will be responsible for subsequent decisions.

Second, one shall not exaggerate evaluations. Padding is considered unethical for a project manager in the professional world, so it is necessary to give a sober assessment of the situation, indicating the range of assumptions. The manager shall look for and find ways to improve the accuracy of the situation analysis. For example, the project can be broken down into several subprojects to work with.

Third, at this stage, the manager is in danger of overdoing it, since we always have more energy at the beginning of the journey than closer to the end. One shall be determined, but feel the moment when it becomes necessary to step back. All the conditions that the manager puts forward and all his requirements shall be justified.

The initiation stage is important and difficult, the success of the entire project depends on it. As they say, to start is half a job, but there is still a lot ahead, as we will describe in the following chapters.

CHAPTER 4

PROJECT SCOPE

The scope formation stage is as important to a project manager as the others. To ignore it means to break the logical link between all stages of project implementation. In this chapter, we will analyze what this phase involves and how to get through it correctly so that all the tasks are successfully implemented.

Identification of stakeholders

We start by identifying the stakeholders interested in the project's success. In the chapter on initiation, we discussed people dealing with our undertaking for different reasons. At this stage, our task is to collect all the names, analyze stakeholder information, and compile a register of people interested in the project.

Stakeholders are all those on whom the project depends in one way or another. This should include everyone from implementers, team members and ordinary staff to people in senior positions.

A stakeholder does not necessarily have to work on the project. If he or she gets any benefits after the project, it means that he or she cares whether or not you manage to bring it to a successful conclusion. And it means that you can count on him in certain situations.

The Stakeholder Analysis Matrix is a list of names of those involved in or benefiting from the project.

At the initial stage, it may seem that you remember all the people involved in the project, with all their merits and contacts. However, over time some information begins to slip out of sight, which is perfectly normal, and then the problem arises: who and how to contact. Each person is a resource, sometimes with a specific function, and the project manager needs to keep this in mind. With stakeholder intelligence, you will work in a more organized way, be able to delegate authority, get the right people and support, if necessary.

In constructing the matrix, the project manager should specify selection criteria – whether the person is on the work plan implementation or can change events, has the authority or important competencies, and his interest in the project. By constructing the matrix, the manager will understand how he or she needs to interact with stakeholders, what information to share and how to do it.

For a more comprehensive stakeholder analysis you should divide them into two main groups. The first would include those directly involved in the project – internal project stakeholders: team members, management, the project manager himself, and specialist groups that deal with the project main tasks. The second group, respectively, would include those not directly involved in the project – these are investors, contractors, suppliers), etc.

With the Stakeholder Analysis Matrix data available, you can start managing your stakeholders. The manager will be able to set up a convenient schedule for everyone, scheduling dates for reporting to some stakeholders and deadlines for receiving performance data from others. Management also includes dealing with expectations (discussed below), allocating people according to their specialization and "pinning" them to the project stages where they contribute to the success.

It is important to keep all the people involved in your task informed and get the necessary feedback.

What is a project scope?

Budding project managers are often convinced that paperwork is a waste of time, which is always in short supply. They prefer to focus their efforts on vigorous action, leaving paperwork "until later". This approach to project management is flawed, and here's why.

Before realizing any idea – to build a kennel for a stray dog, for example – you should visualize the end product in your mind, and in as much detail as possible. Then you should make a drawing of the kennel and choose the materials. And only then can you start building a home for your dog.

The same works for any other project: space, commercial, government. First, the manager and stakeholders visualize the end result in their imagination, then they prepare to implement the conceived idea, defining timing, volumes, necessary technologies, materials, and so on and so forth. All this is put into the scope. Then they get down to business.

The project scope is closely linked to the documents that the project manager, sponsor and team, prepared at the initiation stage. It includes a detailed description of the project itself, as well as the resulting product.

The project scope should include basic information about the project, but what exactly? This will become clear after the project manager and stakeholders have decided on the answers to a number of basic questions while working on the scope.

For instance:

- what are the exact goals and tasks of the project to be implemented?

- what are the resulting product qualities?

- what technologies will the specialists rely on to implement the project?

- what are the project scope, its exceptions and assumptions?

Assumptions, possible risks, boundaries or limitations cannot be ignored, they shall be studied and analyzed. This is why these are taken into account during scope development and then refined as necessary.

Not only the team, but also the customer, the sponsor and the executing company's management shall be involved in the project – this is a joint stage.

The manager should enter a product description, its qualities and characteristics, paying particular attention to the criteria according to which the product will be recognized as a project product.

The project scope is essential to the continuation of work, as it articulates the final task, the goal that the team and other stakeholders will strive for.

It has three useful features.

The scope is all-encompassing – that is, it covers the entire project with all its specificities.

The second quality of the scope is that it is **easy to understand, or simplifies difficult issues**. This document makes it clear how, by what means, and with what technology the goal will be achieved. A detailed understanding of all project mechanisms simplifies work. In seeking additional investment or to form a positive public opinion of the project, project managers and executives often have to describe the project to outsiders. Having the project scope makes this task much easier.

The scope can be useful even after the project has been implemented. It can be used for subsequent projects in the same area on a tried and tested basis.

The scope development phase is divided into three main parts:

- a set of requirements,

- project scope description,

- work breakdown structure (WBS) development.

Let us analyze them in detail.

—ℓℓ—

Requirements gathering

Let's start with the basic concepts: "expectations" and "requirements".

Expectations are not only found in project activities, they accompany our lives since birth in many life situations. Let's say a project manager's mother expected her son to become a famous violinist. And the project manager himself, starting the project, hopes that he will be able to create something that will make happy all the people in the world happy. All stakeholders expect something good from the project (usually money or other benefits). The reason is that the human brain draws a beautiful picture to make the body act, and this has to be reckoned with.

Thus, expectations in project management can be described as a kind of wish or assumption about how the project will be implemented and what kind of product it will bring to market.

People in general, both professionals and ordinary people, always compare the result to what they expected to get. If the first differs from the second for the worse, they are disappointed. There's a reason there are so many "expectation versus reality" memes on social media!

When we dream of something infeasible, we just talk ourselves into "getting your hopes up", but in project management, a tool called expectation management is used to manage inflated expectations. The manager should be good at that, otherwise, he will be to blame for the failure to invent the perpetuum mobile once again.

So, expectation management is about adapting the customer's assumptions to the real world. It demands a good understanding of the project environment. Let's say you know the dollar to euro exchange rate, the price of fuel, the laws of the country where project works will be performed, the technologies applied. During these works the manager affects the expectations of the customer, partner and sponsor. Perhaps it keeps them grounded and warns about the likelihood of related problems.

What methods are used? The most diverse, depending on the situation. The main thing is that the conversation should be based on the mutual respect principles, its purpose is not to destroy all expectations, but only to adjust to reality.

A project is considered successful if the customer is satisfied with the results. That is, when their expectations are met, they have no complaints, and they are happy with the resulting product. Thus, if a manager is aware of exactly what the customer's assumptions about the project result look like, it will be easier for him to adjust those nuances of expectations.

As far as requirements are concerned, these are the customer's practical wishes on which all project plans are based. The manager should understand, identify the main ones and manage as the project progresses.

—ele—

Requirements gathering methods

It would seem that at the first project stages the customer voiced his wishes, so what else? It's time to start implementing the plan! No, it's too early yet. Prior to the first works it is necessary to list and comprehend the customer's requirements once again because now that the preliminary documents have been signed and the project has taken shape in the minds of performers, sponsor and other stakeholders, it's time to make sure of full mutual understanding with the customer.

By this stage, we have the charter, the scope and some other basic documents that we can and should rely on when requirements are gathered. Perhaps it is not necessary to spend much on gathering requirements – specify the customer's main wishes, achieving an understanding of your tasks. Sometimes it is enough to talk to the customer about his dreams and fantasies – and a lot will become clear. However, the larger the project, the longer the requirements gathering period is.

It often happens that the customer himself is not quite sure of his requirements or cannot convey them in clearly. Then he should be offered several options to decide what he wants to see as a result. To gather requirements, you can use several tools and combine them.

The primary method is a simple **interview** on issues developed by the project manager. The customer expresses his wishes in detail and the manager clarifies incomprehensible points. The advantage of this method is in personal, more free communication.

The interview can be recorded as a video or audio file. If a detailed text is written on the interview results, it is recommended to ask the customer to reread and approve it.

A **questionnaire** is an effective requirements gathering method, but the questions should be formulated in such a way that the customer understands them and answers in detail, not "yes", "no" or "I don't know".

In cases where the customer wants to work through and clarify his requirements, it makes sense to offer a brainstorming session, if necessary together with the whole project team. The customer will get help, see the experts in action and have their first exchange of experience.

Reliance on ready-to-use sources

Sometimes the customer already has some experience with projects in the same area, and if they have relevant documents on past ventures, it is worth examining them and finding relevant requirements for your particular project.

Capturing requirements in a matrix

To capture the requirements, a special Requirements Traceability Matrix (RTM) is used, where you can reflect and trace the required parameter changes. The requirements matrix is also called a traceability matrix.

The matrix is necessary to make the project more transparent to the customer, who can specify or add requirements, and all of them will be taken into account, as the matrix allows you to see all the tasks without missing something significant.

The requirements matrix forces the implementers to return to the customer's tasks, and not to let their thought fly because "it's better this way". If there is still a need to improve some working points, the matrix will show how the change will affect the next steps. This tool will also save the project history – perhaps it will come in handy for future achievements.

It is worth noting that in project management, the term "requirements matrix" is more commonly used than the more familiar "terms of reference" (ToR). In the context of project implementation, it is much more convenient to use a matrix, as it is a living and changing document, and the ToR is formed once, at most a new task is written if the old one is no longer workable.

Thus, the requirements matrix is a convenient kind of document, thanks to which the implementer understands his tasks.

Balancing of requirements

Balancing in project management refers to the process of selecting those requirements that will be fulfilled as the project progresses. The first thing to do is to select the requirements that cannot be avoided, i.e. the main requirements.

The next stage is to select from the main ones those that fit into the project framework, into its triangle.

At the requirements stage, the project manager does not yet have exact numbers or final plans, although they are already much closer to reality than before. He will have to use his experience or find specialists to help navigate the current situation. This part of the plan, based on a rough estimate, will still be finalized later when the manager is more confident in his data.

In doing the balancing, the manager will make appropriate notes in the requirements matrix and then sign off on the data with the stakeholders.

Formulating the project scope description

The project scope concept is a detailed and structured description of the project scope. Based on the definitions given in the PMI PMBoK, the document includes a list of activities to make the intended project a reality.

Scope management is the monitoring of changes in the project status and adjustment of corresponding items in the plan. This process always reflects the changes that occur as the project evolves, and if we forget to capture them, we get a "project scope", meaning scope violation. This is wrong, as the project "loses ground".

At predetermined dates, the project scope should be confirmed by the customer, the sponsor or all supervisors. This is a rather formal report, but it allows you to check once again the accuracy of all project deadlines and parameters. The scope can be informed in parallel to the quality control because they are different processes and do not interfere with each other.

Work breakdown structure, or WBS

A fairly important stage in an organizational sense is the development of a work breakdown structure, which breaks down or decomposes project results and the work into smaller parts. The lower in breakdown structure the work, the more detailed it is described in WBS. Decomposition is performed with both final and intermediate activities. In each case, the number of hierarchical levels will be different, as each project has its own individual scope, depending on complexity, duration, work order and a variety of other factors.

Parts of the activities or WBS components that are higher in the hierarchy are called summative; those that remain at levels below are subordinate.

The structural model that the project manager receives as a result of his efforts will be very useful to him for further planning of the work as well as implementation monitoring. With a WBS, you can plan the most important project data, such as costs, deadlines and volumes, which make up the project triangle.

Here are some basic rules for WBS formation:

- Summative components rely on subordinate components.

- A subordinate component is only linked to one summative component.

- The sum of the components has a meaningful result.

- All components are unique.

- The breakdown of works shall include all project activities, and what is not included is not considered to be declared for implementation.

The depth of decomposition is also determined by the following rules:

-

All tasks should be between eight and eighty man-hours, i.e. they should take between one and ten days to complete.

- All tasks should be completed in a period longer than the time between meetings.

- Tasks are decomposed for three reasons:

- they are easier to evaluate,

- they are easier to allocate,

- they are easier to monitor.

———ℓℓ———

In this way, we managed to overcome the stakeholder identification stage, gather the requirements, form the scope and create a breakdown structure of the activities. However, the project's end is still a long way off!

CHAPTER 5

— ⚬ —

TIME PLANNING

With the requirements matrix in place, the project manager can move on to managing the scope as well as clarifying the timing and cost of the project. In other words, it's time for detailed planning of all sides of the project triangle, and we'll start with the "Time" edge.

———*ell*———

Ordering

At this stage, the project manager reverts to the breakdown structure of works, i.e. the WBS, which makes sense, as this complex structure was not created for nothing, but for work. In the previous chapter, we discussed the need to develop a WBS and determined that it reflects the decomposition of works, i.e. the breakdown into smaller goals, and is results-oriented. At the previous stage, the manager has structured the necessary supplies in the WBS and has received visual information ready for further use.

It is worth remembering that a WBS is developed with the team! The involvement of the specialists will help to increase the credibility of the plans and reduce the risk of losing important processes and data needed to implement the project. The joint work will definitely bring the team together.

Once the project manager has determined what shall be done to produce the final product, he or she can start ordering. It requires a logical sequence of tasks and specification of dependencies. The work will not seem too difficult if you have a good understanding of the technologies to be used to implement the project, and of the priorities of the work to be done.

The task order demands that each successive operation logically follows from the previous one, generating at the same time a subsequent operation. The only exceptions are the first and the final operation, since the initial operation has no preceding link and the final operation has no subsequent link. The manager shall understand the logic of this sequence, as he is the one who has to control each stage of project implementation. He or she should see which process has generated the next one, and where the whole chain of operations will lead to in the end.

PERT chart

For successful work, visibility is required, and it can be obtained by translating information from a table into a graphical form. As a result, the manager who has done this work will have a so-called network diagram.

A network diagram in project management is called a PERT chart - Program Evaluation Review Technique.

It is important to know that there is a technique and a PERT chart, and they should not be confused.

When we imply the technique, we are describing the way in which a manager and his team create a PERT chart. And the chart of the same name represents the result of this work – a handy and practical tool used in project management to achieve three main goals:

- planning of forthcoming tasks,

- organization of team works and involvement of stakeholders,

- distribution of tasks amongst those

involved.

A PERT chart contains important data about a project, including such a parameter as the schedule of upcoming activities, reflecting the relationship between tasks and the time needed to complete them. We (or the manager in charge of the project) do not yet have the most precise and verified time frame at this stage. But all the necessary dates will be given soon. This is what the next section of the current chapter is about.

Time frame definition

Before the time frame is set, the project manager allocates responsibilities by assigning people to tasks. It is crucial for professionals working in the same team to understand their responsibilities. Each participant in the work process should be prepared for the upcoming workload, for the level of tasks, and for their roles in the overall action. A lot depends on the proper distribution because everyone is different and everyone has strengths and weaknesses. If this is taken into account, many human factor problems can be avoided in advance.

The assignment of responsibilities precedes the definition of a time frame for the implementation of the project tasks, also because the implementers work at a different pace. If a person in charge has already been appointed, he or she will say how long it will take to complete the task so that the outcome is of high quality. In any case, his or her opinion on the deadline should be taken into account.

While working on the project charter, the manager has already written down the first ideas about the deadlines, but this is not enough now. The data provided at this stage will be the basis for the project's further implementation.

There are many methods in project management to estimate the time required to implement project parts. We will select a few of the most effective ones.

Expert review

It is evident that this type of time expenditure involves people who have expertise in the subject and can support their conclusions. Let's say our project is to build a house and the manager engages a walling expert to say how long it takes to build a five-storey structure. If you want the time frame to be as precise as possible, it makes sense to invite more than one expert.

Three-point estimation

This method is very simple and does not deny the involvement of experts, but this time we will not work with one figure, but with three:

- The first figure is denoted by the letter O, from the word "optimistic". It embodies the best possible scenario for a project or a project stage.

- P (from the word pessimistic) is a number reflecting a scenario built on the assumption that things will go wrong.

- M, or most likely, is the middle option that lies in between.

Based on three figures, the project manager uses the formula $(O + 4M + P)/6$. Once the calculation is done, he will get a figure that takes into account all the options – successful, unsuccessful and intermediate.

Estimation by analogy

The project manager can use this option if he or she has data on a similar project or if he or she has already implemented a similar project and knows the problem like the back of his or her hand. When relying on this method, you should be careful to consider what the differences are between the work on a new project and the work we are using.

Parametric estimation

A complex but also a more accurate method of estimating the project time range. It is based on the construction of a parametrized model of the forthcoming plan, based on available data. The mathematical prediction that this estimation method eventually produces allows for the inference of time expenditure, and will also show the correlation between final and baseline figures. Parametric estimation is convenient in that it allows you to work with margins of variation in the data, so it is very popular in project management.

Bottom-up

This method allows for flexible time frames, as it is based on the sum of estimates of the project parts. It is useful when the project has already been decomposed and the project manager has data on the individual parts of the whole, so that each activity can be timed and then the whole model can be assembled.

Having several techniques for project time data allows for a combination of different estimation methods, which will eventually produce an accurate time frame. If competent experts are available, you cannot refuse their help, but it is also worth using data from similar projects, three-point estimation, etc. Time is a very important resource and should be considered seriously.

—— *ele* ——

Gantt chart

An essential and useful tool for presenting a project visually, assessing relationships and the resource base of tasks, is the Gantt chart. One of the founders of scientific management, Henry Gantt, developed this type of bar chart back in 1910 and since then his invention has been used successfully by professionals in many industries.

A Gantt chart is a schedule of project activities, laid out according to a project plan, showing project tasks themselves and their sequence. It also takes into account data such as the timing of activities, their start and completion dates, and information about responsible people.

The chart is drawn on a time axis, along which the sections corresponding to the planned tasks are placed. Each segment begins on the task start date on the time axis and ends on the completion date. The duration of work to be done, as you can easily guess, corresponds to the length of this segment.

Using this chart, the project supervisor, manager, sponsors, and team members can see how the tasks are distributed, who is responsible, and whether they overlap in time, as well as present an accurate picture of how and when the project will be implemented.

The chart gives a clear picture of the positioning of segments, which allows you to decide in advance whether it makes sense to combine them or, on the contrary, to separate them in time. In this way, work planning becomes a simple matter.

So, with the above tools, the project manager can set a starting point and see if he or she and his or her team are on track to meet the deadlines laid down in the charter.

The project schedule is made even more manageable by adding project milestones, or checkpoints that show, in chronological order, the beginning and end of important activities or project stages. Milestones are markers that are essential to the project's progress, which the manager can refer to as the project progresses. Important milestones can include a schedule for communicating with the customer and providing them with interim reports. You will find that working according to milestones is quite convenient.

However, even if milestones are easily accommodated in the schedule, it is too early to rejoice: in our lives, the ideal is a rarity...

Network-based schedule analysis

A comprehensive method of generating a schedule model in project management is called network-based schedule analysis. Using the Gantt chart and other tools described above, the project manager can anticipate some of the difficulties that await the project in the near future, and make necessary adjustments at a time when it is still possible.

Network-based schedule analysis is a sophisticated approach employed in creating a project schedule model that incorporates multiple techniques. Let's discuss some of them.

1. Resource analysis and leveling

Resource overload is one of the pitfalls that can suddenly become a big problem. When a manager notices that specialists are working irrationally or finds other difficulties, he or she can equalize resources – reorganize the plan so that there is no overload.

Resource leveling can be done in several ways.

Resource load limitation. This method will inevitably affect task duration. That is, if an employee spent eight hours a day on a task and was due to complete it in a week, he will only complete it in a fortnight if he switches to a four-hour working day.

Changing the network-based work schedule. Suppose the Gantt chart shows that one of the resources performs several tasks in the same period, which reduces its efficiency in all directions. A manager can transform the chart by replacing simultaneous tasks with sequential tasks. In this case, each task will require more time allocated to the project.

Resource reinforcement. The manager directs additional resources to one or more concurrent tasks, involving those employees whose tasks have already been completed by this project stage, or hiring new specialists. This way is more expensive, so you will have to reconsider the project budget. By hiring free specialists, the manager risks the quality of work performed, because the original choice of the responsible person was based on his competence, and whether the second responsible person will be as professional – it is still a question.

Introduction of breaks. Breaks in overlapping tasks will free up resources and cancel overlapping tasks, which will reduce the entire system overload. Breaks are extra work hours, so you will have to decide if you can save time on something else, or if you will have to reconsider the time frame for project completion.

Introduction of overtime hours. This is an option not traditionally resorted to by the smartest managers and used to its full potential. However, overtime can be an option in cases where you need to meet a deadline – and that's all! When deciding to work overtime, managers must realize that it is an exceptional decision because it is impossible to work constantly in "go-go-go" mode – employees will quickly become exhausted and start making one mistake after another.

2. Critical path analysis

There is a concept in project management called the Critical Path, readily seen on a Gantt chart. It reflects the sequence of tasks, or sometimes a single task, that determines project duration. The critical path increases, the project completion time goes up, if it shortens, the project approaches completion faster. When analyzing the critical path, the project manager can check if the project deadline is correct and if there is no possibility to shorten the critical path and get the product sooner.

To do this, he or she should analyze several options.

For example, choose the earliest possible start and completion dates for each operation. This data depends on the execution of previous operations and the deadline for a particular task. By adding up the operation start date and task duration, the manager gets the completion date of the operation.

Similarly, the most recent completion dates are determined, i.e. those dates after which work can no longer be started. They coincide with project deadlines.

In this way, we can detect critical operations – their earliest and latest start and finish dates coincide. Critical operations determine the critical path. The earliest due dates of operations indicate the minimum project duration, and the latest due dates indicate the maximum project duration.

3. Schedule crashing

Schedule crashing has the goal of speeding up project work. Crashing is the reduction of the project time frame after analyzing alternatives that could reduce time expenditure without increasing costs or compromising the original product quality. The most balanced options in this sense should be taken into consideration.

4. Fast Tracking

So-called Fast Tracking involves combining, overlapping, or running project phases in parallel to reduce time expenditure. For example, sometimes project managers combine design and construction. Fast Tracking implies a risk of quality degradation.

5. Monte Carlo Analysis

When analyzing the schedule and calculating the project's total cost, a manager can use a Monte Carlo analysis. It takes its name from the associations that arise when this place is mentioned, namely the casino, where so much depends on the probability of winning.

The analysis is built on input data after the study of probability distributions, possible costs, or timing. With the Monte Carlo method, you get probable data about the project cost and the range of completion dates.

To determine project duration, the manager chooses three timing options: the best, the worst and the most probable scenarios. By analyzing resources, team skills, technology, and other factors, he or she determines the percentage probability that each of the scenarios will become real. The manager also considers the duration of project tasks and calculates the likely time frame for their completion.

There can be quite a lot of tasks – dozens or hundreds – and figures on them need to be taken into account, so before computers were invented, this type of analysis was considered very complicated.

The analysis involves multiple (thousand-plus options!) simulations of all possible options, each of which yields a project completion date. In this way, the manager obtains a probability curve that shows different dates of project completion and the percentage probability corresponding to these dates. The date with the highest percentage probability can be considered the most accurate and is taken into account.

The Monte Carlo method is also suitable for the analysis of other indicators. Project budget, for instance.

Monte Carlo analysis provides the necessary statistics to allow for many different variations of the project schedule.

ele

Final Version of The Project Schedule

Schedule Cutting

Sometimes a manager is tempted to simply cut some tasks out of a project so as not to risk the project deadline. You lead and manage, so it's within your power to do this, but never make this decision secretly from the team and stakeholders.

Even if you have all the necessary leverage in your hands, you should never forget that the project is always in the customer's interest. When a manager sees that his or her network analysis does not allow the team to achieve a realistic schedule with a predetermined handover date and without compromising the final product, they should communicate this to the customer and discuss options for resolving the impasse in their common brainchild, the project.

Think of a project triangle, in which changing one side involves changing the other sides. Negotiate, offer to increase the project deadline, or ask for a waiver to cut back on some of the work.

It's a good time to remind the customer that the estimates set before were crude, approximate estimates. If you know you have been hasty in stating a deadline, acknowledge your mistakes. The key to a good relationship with a customer is honesty and transparency.

Final Schedule

VALENTYN BANNIKOV

The result of our work is a realistic schedule, which doesn't contradict the charter, and by which the team is ready to deliver on schedule.

—ele—

And so we worked out the due dates for the project tasks and got a final schedule of upcoming activities. One more step towards the project implementation has been taken!

CHAPTER 6

—·—

COMMUNICATION TO PLAN FOR

People are social beings. The fate of all endeavors depends on how well one employee understands another, which is why project management places great emphasis on the issue of successful communication. Well-established communications will help the manager effectively lead the project to implementation. Below you will learn what actions he should take at the next steps.

—*ele*—

Importance of Communication

Communication issues are often underestimated because it is considered that excessive talking only harms the cause. But not all talk about a project gets in the way of work. If you, as a project manager, get your staff into the habit of communicating regularly and effectively, focusing on what is important and leaving out the unnecessary, then the project process will run smoothly.

For example, the first project team had a meeting once a week and the team of the second, a competing project, had one every day. The first group, noticing any shortcomings and problems, had to wait a week to discuss them with their colleagues, while the second group did not wait, but dealt with all difficulties as they arose. In the end, under equal conditions, the first team lost out by failing to implement the project on time.

Communication is important when presenting a project, engaging public opinion, and building loyalty from company employees or potential consumers of a future product. It is essential to be able to reach an understanding with the investors of the future project, as well as with people who can patronize the project at its implementation stages. An accessible and clearly worded message, press release or presentation can do all these things and more.

What is there to recommend? Use the right words, project managers!

It is a fact that communication of all kinds takes up to 95 percent of a manager's working time, but why so much? First of all, because communication management activities are part of the execution group, which means the following: the manager must perform all necessary actions in this direction himself, not delegating, and not entrusting these duties to anyone else.

Many inexperienced managers complain that they have to hold a briefing, communicate directly with each contractor and report to the customer, while there is still something to be done in the project! They feel that too much communication is detrimental to their direct responsibilities. Such thoughts must be put out of your mind so that they do not interfere with communicating successfully with everyone in your plan, otherwise, you will fail. By the way, it is time to discuss planning verbal interactions.

Communication Should Be Planned Too

When formulating project plans, the manager represents not only the project stages and technologies, but also the people with whom he or she will have to communicate in the near future. Draw up a communication plan, including the structure of the upcoming communication and its forms, in writing, without relying on your superpowers and super memory. The finished document should be presented to stakeholders for them to make adjustments and sign off on. Let everyone involved in the project be prepared for exactly how communication will be structured during the project period.

The communication plan contains an extensive list of items:

- the data of the employees working on the project;

- the information to be communicated;

- quality requirements for all parties involved in the communication process (response times, wording of messages, and so on);

- the way the information will be transmitted.

This list can be supplemented and modified by the manager, depending on the tasks set for him or her.

The communication plans of different projects always vary, as they depend on the conditions in which the project is implemented. Sometimes a manager can make do with an informal outline plan – a "reminder" – for those cases when there is no time or possibility to keep in mind additional volumes of information, and other times a serious step-by-step plan with many explanations is required.

It goes without saying that this plan is not just for show and shall be regularly followed and the results analyzed.

Communication Channels

An important bonus that a manager gets from communications management is understanding the relationship between the size of the team and the number of communication channels. Sometimes it seems that if you get everyone in the office at a difficult task, things will go faster. But the larger the team, the more often people communicate (sometimes for no business at all!), and any project has a deadline to meet.

There are many projects, all of them are different, so it is quite difficult to give recommendations on how many people should be united into a team so that the "communication/work" ratio maintains a perfect balance. In some cases, managers use a concept such as a manageability threshold, it usually implies that the team should consist of seven to nine people. Once the group is slightly larger, communication becomes redundant, taking time away from work processes.

To calculate the optimal number of employees needed to perform a particular job, project managers use another specific concept – "the number of communication channels". Let's say you need to calculate how many people to combine into a team to solve a particular problem. Take the Project Management Knowledge Handbook, which we have already mentioned many times, and use the formula it suggests to solve this question.

According to the formula, the total number of communication channels is $N(N-1)/2$, where N is the number of project participants.

Let's say you recruit a team of four people, and then you have six communication channels. A group of ten specialists will make forty-five communication channels, which can already cause some difficulties. A thorough planning of the interactions will help to avoid them, so that each member of the team will communicate with those with whom they share common tasks.

You can refer to the above formula in all cases when you form a work group. For example, using the crashing technique used as one of the schedule management techniques. Remember that group communication management plays a huge role in work processes, affecting the quality of work and the time it takes to complete a work task.

Types of Communication

The techniques of effective communication are dealt with in detail in the standard course "General Management", so while working on a project, specialists in this field have no difficulty with the choice of types of information transfer.

The only thing that complicates project management is time constraints, so each participant in the project must be clearly aware of his place, the extent of responsibility and limitations. He is also required to execute tasks accurately and quickly, and to meet quality standards. Only communication can bring him all of these conditions, and only constant interaction can avoid problems associated with misunderstanding. The task of the project manager is to get a response from the employee, confirming that he is fully in the situation and is ready to work feats.

Oral and Written, Formal and Informal

As in everyday life, communications differ in their form.

Oral communications are effectively used for discussions, exchanging opinions, making preliminary predictions, and for motivating employees using words. A minor question or problem is also solved verbally.

Written communication is good in that the project manager can record the essence of the problem and the model of its solution that emerged during the discussion. Documents with information that a person's memory can miss or distort (lists, data, contacts) are better kept in writing.

Both methods can be combined. Let's say you talked to someone on the phone, and then exchanged links, phone numbers, addresses, and so on via messenger.

Formal communication is acceptable in a working environment, whether it is written or oral. It is devoid, if possible, of an emotional component and is perfect for communicating facts. Formal communication implies a respectful attitude to all participants in the conversation, correspondence, etc., and also excludes flippant treatment, slang, and foul language.

Informal communication – free communication, in which the frameworks are built by the participants themselves. In informal communication is more personal, and emotions are possible, but the respect for the interlocutor should remain at the same level as in formal communication.

Formal communication disciplines employees and maintains the service hierarchy and a smooth emotional background. An informal communication can sometimes help the project manager to emphasize the importance of the task, and his belief in his employees: "Friends, we've got to get this project done at any cost!" This kind of emotional outburst will be remembered.

Push, pull, interactive communication. There are three basic types of communication in project management.

Push communications serve only to broadcast an idea without a response to it. For example, a press release or announcement.

Pull communication involves selecting information from a database or source, a resource. If a manager has to collect data, he uses this type of communication.

Interactive communication, as the name implies, involves an active exchange of opinions, discussion, general conversation, where everyone hears and perceives the other.

One of the manager's tasks is to ensure that communications are optimally effective for all stakeholders.

——*ele*——

Communication Structure

Communication processes comprise several basic stages: encoding information, transmitting, receiving, decoding. By coding, we do not mean, of course, spy encryption, but recording information, i.e. transforming it into a form that can be transmitted to the recipient. Let's say in the form of an email.

The manager should be mindful of the stages of communication, if only because if there is a breakdown he needs to figure out at what stage the breakdown occurred and how to fix it.

—ℓℓ—

How To Make Communication As Effective As Possible

Response

As a manager who has to communicate with a team, a customer, and a sponsor, it is helpful to develop communication skills. These skills will help to win the interlocutor's trust and willingness to cooperate. Learning how to communicate effectively is not difficult if you really intend to listen and understand the person you are talking to, but if you are deeply uninterested in everything he says, then attempts to portray attention will lead to a collapse.

Respect for the other person's speech can be expressed verbally: "Good idea!", "Yes, I agree!", "I'm sure you understand the issue". Psychologists use this type of support for the interlocutor – they repeat the end of the sentence and agree with it or ask a clarifying question: "So, you say you can do this job in two weeks, right? Okay, but what resources will you need?"

The non-verbal expression of attention – a nod of agreement, appropriate gestures corresponding to the words of the speaker. Facial expressions are rather important, so you need to be able to express interest, sympathy, surprise, joy. But the main thing in non-verbal communication is eye contact, your eyes, which you do not take away every two minutes to look at the phone, through the window, or at the girl who passed by.

Optimal Choice of Communication Tools

The choice of communication channel should stem from the project tasks. Let's say the team needs to exchange documents – so it is necessary to find a messenger that makes it possible. In some cases, video communication is necessary, which means you must choose from services that offer it.

In most cases, the team uses e-mail and messenger. The project manager should warn the employees in advance about the rules, which will help not to confuse the files sent in different ways, and require compliance with the rules of business correspondence. You shouldn't allow employees to chat about anything in the work chat room. Communication, as this chapter has already made clear, is a serious matter!

Language and Speech

It may sound strange, but sometimes people do not understand each other simply because they do not want to speak their own language.

A manager cannot hire specialists for a project by offering them a language test and choosing those whose work he wept over in tears. But he can set the level of communication, demanding that everyone in his team not only think clearly but also communicate their insights clearly. At first, the employees, especially their slow-witted part, will be dissatisfied with the constant requirement to express themselves as precisely and clearly as possible, but in time they will get used to it.

Professionals in different industries use jargon, and this too should be taken into account. If not everyone on the team is a programmer, you should make it a rule to avoid terms that confuse the rest of the team. At the same time, if all the specialists are of "the same breed," it does not make sense to forbid them to speak the way they are used to.

Bureaucratic language is a separate topic. For some reason, it is assumed that saying "I am a specialist" rather than "I'm a specialist" sounds cooler. However, the hackneyed linguistic joke about only ghosts being ghosts comes to mind. A penchant for bureaucratic terms makes communication difficult, and irritates some people, leading to a new breakdown in communication.

Communication Management

Management in this case is the work of organizing the information space of a project in which data is exchanged effectively, the progress of the project is discussed and opinions are exchanged.

In the course of his work, the manager maintains necessary resources, provides access to information bases, and controls communication channels. He publishes necessary information about the project and receives feedback from stakeholders.

In project management, there are three important processes associated with communication management: planning, management itself and monitoring. The second and third functions are very close, but not interchangeable. You need to build communication, analyze what you get and, based on the conclusions, build communication again, taking into account amendments.

Reports and Their Types

Work on the project implementation is controlled by the customer and other stakeholders, so it is necessary to make reports. In project management, it is accepted that a report is also a communication.

Reports come in many different forms. You could say that there are as many as there are tasks in the project, because everything the team does, in one way or another, has to be reported on. In order for both the manager and those to whom he or she reports to understand why all these papers, graphs, charts, and tables are needed, project management has developed several basic types of reporting.

Progress Report

In this document, the project manager reports on the project status so far. The progress report contains a situation analysis, so it will require a lot of effort. You will have to make a cross-section of all positions, not missing a single detail. The advantage is that, thanks to several such reports made at different times, you can track the project dynamics.

A status report is almost the same thing, but more superficially, simplified. It may be used if the previous type of report is too voluminous, and the customer does not ask to go into details, wanting to see at what stage of the project today.

A forecasting report is a comparative type of reporting that allows you to see whether there is currently progress in project development or, alas, the team is stagnating and deadlines are going down the drain.

A trend report allows you to understand what awaits the project in the future. This is a rather complex document requiring a manager to have a skill to "look into the future" in the most prosaic sense, of course, by analyzing facts and understanding the essence of emerging trends.

EVA report (EVA stands for "economic value added") is required in order for the manager and all interested parties to have a clear idea of how financially stable the project is and whether there are any problems with payments to creditors.

All of these reports should be filled out and shared with project management in line with the communication plan.

Communication Analysis

It is equally important to analyze the means of communication, as well as to identify those cases where the exchange of information is not effective enough. The manager's main task is to spot and eliminate the cause.

Project Communication Management Techniques

- Conversation. Let's say the manager sees that somewhere there is a communication blockage, and the reason for this is the mood of the people. You should first talk to some team members, listen to what they are dissatisfied with and how they would like to solve the problem, and only take action afterward.

- Research of information systems. Modern Internet messengers, chats and other services designed to communicate, make it possible to superficially track the activities of system users to understand their reactions to communication. Suppose you have your own project chat room, but your employees prefer WhatsApp. Why? There can be many such questions, and the answers to them result in a wide variety of problems.

- Failure analysis. Let's say you notice some problem, and then you find out that the cause is communication. You have to eliminate the cause of what happened and thereby correct the situation. It is important not to let the failure happen again, and to check the communications as often as possible. In serious cases, it is necessary to check the communication plan and modify it accordingly.

———ele———

Well-established communications will help the manager effectively lead the project to

implementation. Below you will learn what
actions he should take in the next steps.

CHAPTER 7

RISK RESPONSE

The way we think about it, the risk is uncontrollable. We only assume that something extraordinary may happen, but we cannot say for sure if it will or will not happen.

At the same time, a professional project manager is competent enough to know where to soften the blow, so why not do it?

What Does It Mean To Manage Risks?

To manage risks means pursuing a proactive policy where we are not flapping our wings after the tsunami that destroyed our project – the house under construction, but anticipating the cataclysm and then proceeding to a well-thought-out plan of action. And flapping wings is reactive politics, by the way.

Risks come in negative and positive forms. The former brings problems, and the latter has positive results. The project manager's task is to reduce the possibility of negative risks or reduce the amount of trouble they will bring. And also, if possible, to increase the chance of positive accidents.

Risk management is based on a certain algorithm, which consists of:

- risk management planning,

- risk identification,

- qualitative risk analysis,

- quantitative risk analysis,

- risk response planning,

- risk response,

- risk monitoring.

The main document where the manager reflects the work with risks is called a risk register. The identified risks, which we will discuss below, are entered into it, it is filled in the columns of the name, description, name of the risk host, developed plan B.

Every project manager knows that any project is a risky business because it is initiated and implemented under conditions of high uncertainty. The first thoughts that both might happen are born at the initiation stage, but they are not included in the algorithm and are not allocated to a separate process. In some cases, risks are included in the project charter, but a serious discussion of the likelihood of risks and the preparation of contingency plans take place much later when all the basic plans are in place.

This is something that is carried through to the end of the project because there is always the risk that the customer will be dissatisfied with the results.

Risk Planning

Risk management planning involves serious reflection on developments in the near future. The activity that mirrors planning is monitoring, where you already know roughly where the trouble is coming from and begin to track it.

Risk management planning starts after the project charter is finalized. The tools and templates to work with at this stage are selected from the assets of the organizational process and the enterprise environmental factors. In the course of work, the manager makes a risk breakdown structure, where he enters all possible types of risks, as well as information about them.

The risks are identified by all stakeholders in the process, as everyone has their own area of tasks in which risks are encountered. The team, the project customer, the sponsor, the manager can organize a brainstorming session to decide which risks are most likely to occur and which of them are worthy of a separate study. There can be several such brainstorming sessions because the number of risks increases as the project progresses. It is reasonable to brainstorm at the project start and then work through the same topic with the stakeholders to clarify the situation.

Contractors can also suggest the likelihood of new risks since they usually specialize in one particular topic and are better versed in it than many other project participants.

Risk Identification

The project manager should understand the risks and determine how serious they are and what they might result in, so he uses the Identify risks technique. It includes different ways of collecting information and analyzing it: meetings, brainstorming, facilitation, which means "process facilitation", as well as the SWOT analysis.

SWOT analysis is based on a matrix with four items:

- Strengths;

- Weaknesses;

- Opportunities;

- Threats.

The capital letters of the names add up to the acronym S.W.O.T.

The positions are arranged in two rows on the chart. The top two – S and W – usually correspond to the situation status, while O and T are the risks. After completing the SWOT matrix, the manager can analyze the situation and forecast its development.

After working through the topic of risk identification, the manager compiles a risk register with basic information about unplanned situations that could harm or contribute to the project. The document will be added to as you go along, until the end.

ele

There Are Different Risks

Having compiled a risk register, the manager begins to realize that his list contains a very wide variety of probabilities that require his attention. There can be so many risks that it is unlikely that even half of them can be prepared for, and we all understand that in terms of percentage probability, most of the risks are minor and some of the work spent on preparation will not pay off anyway. This is why risks are to be classified and prioritized.

To do this, a manager performs a qualitative risk analysis, that is, an analysis of the quality of risks, which allows the selection of the main, the most "terrible", and those that are unlikely to bring serious trouble. The main risks shall be worked on further, and the study of the others can be postponed.

The risks are analyzed by the level of criticality and probability, and assessed according to criteria that relate to customer interests, formal requirements, environmental factors, etc., depending on the project itself.

The most logical way is to draw a timeline and allocate immediate and long-term risks on it, and then periodically work through those probabilities that are looming in the near future.

You can also set a probability criterion and start working through those risks that are most likely to occur.

Risk significance is an important parameter because it is what the manager will be guided by. On closer inspection, not all swords of Damocles are as imminent and dangerous as first thought. When identifying the significance parameter, we should first determine its level:

- high – a category that will have to be dealt with necessarily;

- medium – risks at this level should be kept in mind so as not to miss the moment when their significance increases;

- low – it can be postponed because it is unlikely that these risks will threaten the project.

The manager can then use a tool such as the probability and impact matrix. Experienced managers prefer to work with a table of five columns arranged in two rows. Two additional positions are needed for the following values:

- very high significance,

- very low significance.

Five columns will allow you to distribute risks so that those that fit the "very" parameter never approach the position of average importance, and the manager and his team will not waste time on the probability of an alien invasion or a zombie apocalypse. A joke, of course, but...

———ele———

Quantitative Risk Analysis

It is quite a complicated type of work, not applicable to all projects. This analysis makes it possible to estimate risks in numbers. Its name in the sources is Perform quantitative risk analysis, and it is based on three techniques:

- expert evaluations and brainstorming sessions,

- project management formulas,

- simulation modeling.

Quantitative analysis allows you to calculate the reserves that should be laid down in case of risks, so sometimes it is better to do this analysis, rather than hoping for luck.

The first two techniques are clear, but the formulas and modeling are to be worked out.

Project Management Formula. The expected monetary value, i.e. the impact of EMV risks, is calculated using the formula: $EMV = P \times I$, where P is Probability, the probability in percent, and I is Impact, the impact in money or time.

For example, a project manager is fifty percent sure that a used concrete mixer for ten thousand roubles will break down during work on a skyscraper project. Then he uses the above formula: EMV = 50% x 10,000 = 5,000. It turns out that he has to budget five thousand roubles for this risk.

Why don't we put in the cost of the concrete mixer right away? As it's not just the concrete mixer that is being set aside, but also other risks – weather-related interruptions, rising prices, poor quality building materials, etc. However, not all risks will materialize, so we do not put the full amount into the risk fund for every risk that occurs, but rather refer to the formula given above.

Simulation Modelling Or Decision Tree

There is another way to assess risks. For this, we take a piece of paper and a pen. We put a reference point or our decision, and then draw a multi-step probability diagram based on the following principle: if we do this, we get this, and if we refuse, we get that. The goal is to calculate the probabilities all the way to the bottom line and figure out in the end whether this decision is worth taking or how serious this particular risk is. The tree makes it possible to eliminate the emotional underpinnings of the discussion because you're only working with the actual decision.

Quantitative analysis results in another update of the risk register.

Problem List

Parallel to the work we talked about above, the project manager should work through such a notion as a problem list, which turns the realized risks into. In this case, we already mean real facts, not probabilities. And this list includes only negative events that have had an impact on the project.

This document is interesting because thanks to it a manager can test his skills in identifying possible risks by analyzing the problem list after the project is completed. By recording your own "predictions" that have come true, you can also analyze the efficiency of samples in terms of quality, time, or significance.

Sensitivity Analysis

At this point, it is time to calculate the response of the project's economic indicators to changes in external and internal conditions. For example, how dependent the project is on price increases, restrictions on the supply of certain building materials or other factors.

There are different schemes to assess the sensitivity of the project to changes. In some cases, we focus only on one factor, but if necessary, we can address several. One of the simplest methods is to involve experts in the assessment, although there are others.

The performance indicators for the baseline information are calculated using software products, and then the manager compares the baseline and the resulting scenario. Thus, he sees possible changes in the project indicators and assesses its resilience to various risks.

One of the most effective tools for determining project risk sensitivity is the Tornado diagram. One way to do this is to write down all the negative and positive risks from top to bottom, starting with those that have the maximum impact. The horizontal axis should show the percentage change in project cost. In a more complex variant, the whole set of risks is analyzed, taking into account the positive and negative risks.

The purpose of the diagram is to show how risks will affect the project.

Risk Response Planning

The manager has to calculate how he and his team will act if the envisaged risk becomes a reality. To do this he should go on to complete risk registers on the following items:

- plan A;

- plan B;

- risk trigger,

- risk host.

Plan A

This is called the Contingency plan. It is developed to reduce the likelihood of risk or its negative consequences. In the case of positive risks, we assess the opposite: how to create a favorable situation for the risk and how to increase its positive impact.

In the case of negative risk, Plan A considers several ways in which the situation can evolve.

- Escalation involves turning to senior management to help resolve the problem.

- Evasion avoids deepening the conflict and avoids a negative situation.

- Mitigation is an attempt to negotiate, to resolve the situation for the mutual benefit of all parties.

- Transfer – handing over the task to a doer who will take over the problem.

- Acceptance is the most Buddhist option, involving no action at all.

Sometimes we make a decision in an attempt to avoid risk, but in doing so we cause a secondary risk. For example, we find out that the weather is about to get radically bad and decide to repair the roof as soon as possible. We hire a second crew to do it, but that's a risk because we can't be sure that it will work with the right quality.

Plan B

In project management, Plan B is always a Fallback plan. When we think of a Plan B, we try to find a way out of a negative situation. Maybe we need to step back and repeat some action, but more diligently. Maybe we need new resources or the support of influential people from outside.

Plans A and B differ in the way they are funded. Plan A involves full-scale expenditure, while plan B involves only partial expenditure, calculated according to the formula we know $EMV = P \times I$.

Risk Trigger

It indicates that plan A has not worked and we have to turn to plan B. For example, we find out that a business that we have been working with successfully is closing down. We will have to look for another one, which will result in new costs.

Risk Host

The manager assigns the trigger to a team member who has something to do with the area of possible risk – he becomes the risk host. In practice, everyone on the team can be a response planner, as long as they understand the task and are aware of their responsibilities.

—ele—

Response Plans

Plan A provides the most obvious and cheapest way to respond to risk. If you know that there will be an increase in the price of construction materials in a month, you will not wait for prices to go up, but rather buy everything you need in advance by renting an additional warehouse.

When taking up Plan A, we have to make all necessary adjustments to the WBS and the Gantt chart, because we have had to decide to go beyond the envisaged plan and also spend an extra amount on renting a warehouse.

Sometimes the bad luck is prolonged – the risk owner finds out that there is not enough building material at the base at the price we had budgeted, and then we have to do plan B – order the material from a neighboring town. We buy them at the old price, but pay extra for transportation. In the end, we manage to win on the whole, because if we had waited for the price hike we would have spent a lot more money, but there is still a small overspend.

An important point: the risk host does indeed act in a masterly manner, as he himself gives the command to execute plan B. Only then does he inform the project manager about it. Thus, the project manager's task of delegating his authority is fulfilled, which indicates well-coordinated and thoughtful teamwork.

Risk response belongs to the execution process group, so it is handled by the manager personally. Response implementation starts when plan A is replaced by plan B and the risk host informs the project manager.

Monitoring

It is a process of keeping track of the risks that we have previously identified and put on the register. Some on the list have lost relevance and some have increased in significance. There may be new risks that need to be analyzed.

In the meantime, risk analysis continues – new, unplanned probabilities are entered into the register and analyzed. Such work should not stop for a single day; it is part of risk monitoring.

It is quite common for a risk to suddenly be triggered that nobody had foreseen beforehand.

There is nothing tragic about that, but the team and the project manager will have to make a decision on the fly. The first thing to do, of course, is to assess how much more complicated the project could become due to the situation and then come up with plans A and B as a matter of urgency.

Sometimes a new risk that seems to have popped up from under the ground can cause a shift in the basic parameters of the project triangle. You can use the schedule management tools we discussed in the previous chapter to adjust the changes.

Agile approach to risk management

Not the most common method of teamwork, agile is not so much a technique or a technology as a special, one might say, philosophical approach to project management. The use of agile for work processes justify itself in an uncertain environment where you need a flexible response to changing conditions.

The agile approach is good because specialists working on the project use retrospective discussions, trying to find new, more efficient methods of work. Involvement in the work process pays off. Besides, agile involves constant communication with the customer, adjusting and approving plans, which benefits the project.

Agile is also unique in that each member of the team works in constant working communication with colleagues. By participating in small daily meetings, everyone tells in a nutshell what they are doing and what their immediate plans are, so a common rhythm of work is maintained.

Risks are a topic that is mostly learned by doing, by trial and error. Nevertheless, project management offers effective ways of managing this area of project implementation that should be used.

CHAPTER 8

— · —

PROGRESS MONITORING

In the previous chapters of this book, we discussed what you need to do to arrive at just this very moment – to launch a project. And here we are!

As you have already noticed, preparation takes a huge amount of time, and now that the material part of the work begins, so to speak, the project manager can see that he has not pored over the paperwork, made tables and come up with plans A and B for nothing.

Is it possible to launch a project if you, as a project manager, have missed some stage of preparation?

A rather complicated question, the answer to which depends on the nature of the project itself, the level of specialists involved, and the skill of the manager managing the project himself. Many professionals in this field are renowned for their ability to go through the preparatory stages, as they say, on automatic. They have developed this skill over many years because they have learned from their own, often painful, experience that preparation is a fundamental part of the realization of any important undertaking.

The project is a new phase of work that combines both a management phase and an execution phase, which cannot but increase the project manager's responsibility. Production work will require him or her to focus on controlling and making sure that all activities carried out by the team comply with the plan and timetable.

It may seem that the role of the project manager is no longer as important as it was in the early stages of the project, i.e. there is less running around, people are working, and the PM just reminds them that they have to get there by a certain date. I wish I had something else to do, but I'm wasting my labor force!

This is, of course, a joke, but there is some truth in it, albeit very little – the manager's duties have become a little different after the start of operations. Whereas previously he was in charge of the whole process and the team was just advising him, giving out their thoughts on deadlines, sharing their thoughts on the timing of certain tasks, now it's not like that. The specialists started working at full capacity, while the manager took care of the less visible, to the outsider's eye, tasks.

It should also be understood – for the customer, the project implementation has already started a long time ago, at the moment of preliminary discussion of the idea of the forthcoming business with the manager and other stakeholders. In his mind, there is no fundamental difference between initiation and launch, as they are all only stages of the same work. Let's consider a list of the project manager's main points of application at the start-up stage.

—— *ele* ——

Risk Management

Let's start with what was said before. In the chapter on risk management, we brought up the unpredictability of all of our lives and project activities as well. Unfortunately, all of our plans have one thing in common: sometimes they do not come true. And every plan failure has its own reason, and before it materializes, it was just a risk that could be foreseen. Many risks are very insidious and have a habit of appearing out of nowhere just when you are not expecting them.

That is why a project manager should never lose sight of them.

A risk register will help him in this noble endeavor, so that he can launch Plan B in time. Those risks that no longer seem relevant need to be reassessed in the new environment, as aspects of the team's activities that have already been discussed and deemed irrelevant once can be inadvertently overlooked.

The most sensible approach is to make risk identification a day-to-day task and monitor it in a targeted way.

Change Management

A closely related topic to risk is project change, and it is also worth talking about at the beginning of the start-up stage. First and foremost, change will be inevitable when planning starts to materialize and life makes adjustments to all project work.

Experienced managers know roughly by eye how many changes are not critical for this particular project, and when it is time to sound the alarm. The only criterion that can be used as a guide is the project manager's experience in project management. Sometimes in practice, things unfold that cannot be foreseen in theory. There are times when a project is in jeopardy, even though hardly any changes are required, and sometimes you have to rearrange literally all the plans, but in the end, everything works out and results in a successful delivery of the required product.

To make changes, use a requirements matrix, in which the team members enter their positions, and then the project manager examines the list and draws up his conclusion.

VALENTYN BANNIKOV

It is not easy to assess the feasibility of change, especially when a project manager is facing the need to work with change for the first time. You always have to do something for the first time! There is a very real algorithm for assessing change.

- Find out how well the change fits in with the goals for which the project is being implemented. Does the change bring you closer to getting the product? Then accept it. If not, reject it.

- Check whether the proposed change fits into the triangle and how it will affect the geometry of that figure if we end up accepting it. It may be that by adopting the change, our triangle will start to sprawl, which means that the whole project will be at risk.

- It is important to consider the views of the team, as they will be the ones who will have to put the change into practice. It may be that they will propose to keep the same conditions, but adjust some minor items to leave the plan as it was before the project was launched.

- Check in advance what steps will have to be taken to make the change. Won't there be new risks, schedule compression and other actions that will take up the team's time and energy? If you realize that the change is not worth the effort, it is best to reject it straight away.

- If the change still cannot be abandoned, the project manager will need to alert the customer and possibly anyone else interested in the project. The project's transparency shall remain impeccable from start to finish, and the project manager needs to be on the safe side in case something goes wrong. The decision will also need to be communicated in the event that a decision is made to refuse. Before talking to the customer, prepare arguments in favor of your point of view and provide for possible objections. At this project stage, most PMs are already quite familiar with their customer and can predict the course of his thoughts.

If you follow this scheme or create your own based on it, you will avoid the biggest problem of this stage: the chaos that inevitably arises when an idea collides with real life.

After the launch of a project, as has happened many times in practice, many stakeholders become anxious: is everything provided for, what if we have missed something? "Interesting ideas" start to pop up in their minds, and many have the same feeling "Why didn't we think of this before? " As a result, a bunch of "what needs to be changed right now" ideas are born, and the manager has to deal with it all, whether he wants to or not.

Can a manager say no to a customer, sponsor or someone in management and not accept his change? Yes, if the change starts to distort the shape of the triangle, which is bound to affect the timing of the project, the price or the final product quality. The most important thing in rejection is to justify your decision and to discuss the stated topic in a timely manner.

—ele—

Management of Customer Expectations

This task flows smoothly from the previous one since the discussion with the customer of his proposed ideas is the management of his expectations.

As discussed in the previous chapters, it is necessary to work non-stop with customer expectations from the very beginning of the project. Quite often customers think that the product that the project manager and his team will give them will be a breakthrough in the world of electronics or architecture, or even will change the course of civilization on the planet. The project manager's task is to see reality without rose-tinted glasses and to lower the degree of the customer's rapturous expectations by correlating them with the truth of life.

If a project manager doesn't like to "fiddle with this nonsense", which is quite common, then at the time of project delivery he will get a surprise – an unsatisfied customer. The man dreamed of the Taj Mahal and got a crooked shed on the side of the road! Of course, he is not happy. All you had to do was to discuss his ideas from the start, listen to his wishes and work with his complaints, and then the customer would gradually moderate his appetite and appreciate the shed as the product he was hoping to get.

When working with the customer's expectations, the PM should realize that only he or she has the authority to change his/her mind in this situation. The manager's responsibility for the project is always a hundred percent in the end, which increases his status within the project.

One practical tip that is useful in dealing with customer expectations: when making decisions, always think about the moment of project handover. Keep it in mind, orientate yourself, reduce all your chains of logic to this point, which is still in the foreseeable future. This is the only way to move forward in the shortest possible path and not waste time on idle chitchat.

While respecting the rights and demands of the customer, the PM cannot ignore the wishes of others concerned. They, too, are entitled to their opinions, and these can change considerably as the project progresses, especially at the launch stage.

One of the most important rules is never to refuse feedback, never avoid discussing a problem, and never be perfunctory in your responses to questions and requests.

—ℓℓ—

Work Performance Management

By the time a manager starts, they have a Work Breakdown Structure, plans, a calculated triangle, a timetable for what is to come and a budget. In some cases, PM, having reported these documents to the customer, signed off on them with sponsors, customers and, if necessary, contractors, put the paperwork aside. They justify their actions simply: plans are just fantasies, and once you get down to the real thing, there's no more time for them!

And therein lies a huge mistake. You have to make plans so that they are realistic, and once they are launched, you have to follow them strictly, otherwise you are unlikely to get anything done. The manager has to check on a daily basis how the tasks are being realized and how well this corresponds to the deadlines specified in the project documents.

Specially designed software is used to track progress on some projects, especially IT-related ones, but if there is no need to master this tool and you can mark what has already been done in some other way, it is better to do so.

It is recommended not to delegate this work to someone on the team, as it is useful for the manager to study the data coming from the employees themselves. For example, you could develop a report form for employees to fill in regularly and pass it on to the manager via post or other convenient means.

What is the best way to keep track of the progress of project work?

Practical activity suggests several options.

The first is based on a mathematical calculation. This is the most complicated method, and not suitable for all projects. It should be used in cases where progress cannot be "seen" or "felt". It is also not every team is able to master mathematical methods for tracking progress. Let's say it would not be easy for a construction site foreman to report using this method, so don't force him to.

The simpler method is ratios. For example, when starting a job, your colleague reports: "My progress is 20/80!" That is, the mere fact that he has begun the task already gives him twenty percent of the total. A few days later, he says he's gotten to a 50/50 ratio, which means he's already halfway through the task. And when you get the coveted 100/0 – congratulations on finishing the work. The disadvantage of this method is the uncertainty, but an approximate figure is always better than no data at all.

The most popular method is, of course, the most obvious: the manager interviews or offers to fill in the questionnaire, and the employee describes the status of the task. That's fine! The main thing is for the PM to have time to study the data received.

Progress values need to be analyzed and for this we can use the techniques we have studied in previous chapters. We then check at how well our project is progressing.

It is likely that at some point our triangle will begin to change its proportions. If this is the case, we need to double-check the schedule data to see if there is a mistake. If not, you should reassess the risks, and then you may be able to free up some resources.

We have already discussed the question of whether it is worth adding extra hours to employees, so you are prepared to deal with this issue. We should just add that for many people these days, overworking is not the worst thing a manager can do. They are much more concerned about late payments or being cheated by managers who promise to pay for extra work but later decide not to fulfill the promise. Although the laws are valid, there are always loopholes for company owners to get out of contentious cases. The project manager simply has to take the position of defending the interests of the team or individual specialists, because his or her sacred duty is to motivate the team to do the right thing. A deceived and dissatisfied employee will no longer be willing to work for the same employer who has, quite simply, made a fool of him. A team where no one is going to work full-time is just a group of hired workers who don't care what the final project turns out to be. And if there are problems with the project, only the project manager will be responsible.

Team Management

Now it seems logical to discuss the team and its management.

The main method of work of the project manager in this area is motivation and all available methods. A project manager should have the right to influence salaries and bonuses because it is silly to deny the effectiveness of influence with money! But sometimes money, for all its value, is not as important as self-respect or the opportunity to prove oneself in one's favorite business. It is useful for a manager to know about their people, what they want out of their work and what "carrots" they are willing to try for.

Not all project managers enjoy the role of the amateur cheerleader who organizes corporate parties and outdoor football competitions. If this kind of activity is "against your will", then don't force yourself. Give the job to the most enthusiastic employee. Infrequent but heartfelt celebrations are necessary to strengthen the team.

Another area of teamwork is upgrading of skills. If the project conditions allow, why not provide training that is useful for the business?

It should be discussed in advance with the project investor, and if the investor can be persuaded that staff training is necessary as part of the project, they can be offered some funds for this noble cause. It is also important to choose the right training topic. When working on a pipe-laying project, it is not a good idea to broaden the staff's horizons with lectures on art history, but some innovations in legislation concerning the specific topic of the project will come in handy. After training, don't forget to analyze the results, noting whether team members benefited and were satisfied.

Teams are united by tasks, so involve your specialists in the planning, work breakdown structure and schedules. The more stakeholders put labor into planning a project, the more they will be drawn into it. It is not management who will impose their plans on them, but they themselves will decide how, what and when it will be done. A personal decision will increase their ownership of the project and involvement in everything that happens.

———*ele*———

Reporting on Project Progress

We know that reporting is another integral responsibility of the project manager. Who should he or she report to? Yes, to virtually all stakeholders. But it should not be the same report, like: "Dear friends, it is with a sense of deep satisfaction that I would like to inform you..."

Each report should be prepared individually. It is more important for the customer to know how much progress his project has made. He would also be happy to hear that the deadlines have not been missed and that there are no financial problems. If there is a way to keep him or her out of it, it is better to take advantage of it. There are impatient customers who want to control everything – then go deeper into the report, but towards the positives. It is important to strike a balance when a project manager tries not to withhold information, but at the same time not to voice too much, so as not to arouse nervous curiosity in the customer. It should be remembered that we always stick to management principles when communicating with them, avoiding undue familiarity or bureaucracy.

The manager also reports to the sponsor. When communicating with him as a resource owner, more attention should be paid to the budget, deadlines, interaction with the contractor. The sponsor can solve many problems that arise in the course of the project, so it is necessary to talk about it as often as possible.

In addition to the customer and the sponsor, the project manager's report should also go to the supervisor, if the manager has a supervisor. And you shouldn't withhold progress from your employees. The team also needs to understand how successful their actions are and whether there are any problems that slow down the work.

These are the kinds of tasks that a project manager will perform until the project is handed over. This is what we are going to discuss next.

CHAPTER 9

— ¡ —

SUCH AN IMPORTANT CLOSING PHASE

Final Stage: Banquet or Routine?

Every project has a time limit, so the completion stage is inevitable. People unfamiliar with project management may think that completion is a banquet, salute and brunch with the customer. Practice shows that the closing in such a pleasant form is quite likely, but before this you will have to work hard. The peculiarity of the closing stage is that at the beginning of the phase, the project manager brings all the remaining work to completion and only then begins to prepare the presentation of the resulting product.

Thus, the final stage of the project includes a number of closing processes – this is what we will discuss in this chapter.

The project closing stage should look something like this. At a predetermined time, the project manager informs the customer that the product is ready, and invites him to accept it. After viewing the product, the customer happily admits that he sees exactly what he ordered, and then pays for it. The manager hands him the necessary certificates, instructions, or licenses for the product, and then the project gets closed. This is the pattern, and in reality things may be different.

The things that the manager will do at the closing stage are purely administrative: preparing and drawing up a bunch of different papers, meetings, surveys, working out warranty conditions, organizing the work that needs to be done after the project is completed. Some points in this routine will be boring, but to abandon them is to leave the project incomplete.

If the product involves performance testing, it shall be done then. This compares the planned and actual performance of the product, detects and examines deviations from planned values. When the overall picture is clear, the manager begins to develop a system of measures that will eliminate the discrepancies.

And even after all this work, there are still tasks that need the manager's attention. You would say – the project is completed, the product is received, so what else is needed? It turns out that things are not so simple in project management. At the very end of the closing phase, it is necessary to analyze all the work performed to draw conclusions about each stage passed, about cooperation with the team, about equipment and techniques, if they were used during project implementation.

The analysis of the achieved results is very important for the manager because it opens a great opportunity to work on his or her own competencies. Now that the project is ready for handover, it is possible to understand your actions and even feelings. Evaluate the quality of relationships with the team and other stakeholders. It is time to remember how difficult or easy it was to manage customer expectations, how communication with the sponsor and other project stakeholders was. At the end of the day, it will become clear whether you need to hone your skills in collaboration with your stakeholders. If you take the path of a project manager, you will always have to work with people, which is not easy. Gain experience by learning from both mistakes and successes, and the best period for this is the project completion stage.

An equally important process of the closing phase is debriefing, followed by working on mistakes. All of this should be done as soon as the customer has accepted the project and product. If you postpone these matters until later, you can guarantee with a 98% probability that they will remain in the "Someday Later" folder forever and ever. Over time, we always feel that the stage we have passed is not so important, the project we have completed is not so interesting – we have already learned to do the right thing, and there is never enough time to do all kinds of analyses.

This is what one of the traps of our lazy minds looks like. Avoid it and always evaluate the outcome of each project immediately after handing it in – otherwise, you will miss out on an important experience, which is the most valuable outcome of any life event.

Early Project Completion

Much more desire to understand what was done wrong and why mistakes were made, occurs in the case if the project was not as smooth as expected, or at early completion of the project.

This is not to say that early completion of a project is an outlier. Such things happen quite often because, as has been said many times in this book, it is impossible to guarantee the outcome of a project, and this is one of the axioms of project management.

Project management identifies four main options for project completion.

Completion According To a Set Deadline. The most perfect scenario is to close the project on January 15, and you close it on that date, and not one hour later.

Early Completion

This is a classic scenario where something didn't quite go as expected before. There can be many reasons for this. For example, a mistake in planning, or a change in circumstances – an unexpected price increase, an order that was unexpectedly canceled by the client, and so on.

Often the early completion is caused by a failure in risk handling, in which case it is the personal fault of the PM or the risk host. In rare cases, early completion is not due to mistakes or changed circumstances, but because the project manager was able to build the work more efficiently than originally intended. In fact, it is also a planning mistake, but with a plus sign.

Completion With a Floating Deadline

It would seem that the project has already reached the final stage, but it goes on and on. This is mostly what happens when there are glitches in several stages of planning and a number of small mistakes are made. They don't disappear into thin air but accumulate, and the unfortunate consequences only resurface by the time the project is delivered.

Another option is errors in managing customer expectations when at the very end of the work the customer unexpectedly asks to modify a detail of the product, which he had not thought of before, and which was not included in the plan. Should you tell him to accept the project and not be capricious, because he himself signed project statutory documents, or still accept his requirements and start executing his wishes? In the first option, you will complete the project on time, and perhaps you will receive an additional small order to finalize the product under the new conditions. If you choose the second option, you will get a long-term project completion.

Completion Due To Force Majeure

The case that no one can foresee in advance. Of course, every contract mentions circumstances that can lead to project failure, but no one really thinks about such things, and so they always happen unexpectedly.

The project completion process establishes procedures that investigate and document the reasons for actions taken if a project is closed before completion.

Early project completion can take the form of liquidation and occur while the product is still in the works. Let's say a construction company dug the foundation, erected the structure of a future building, and went bankrupt. In this case, the construction will go under the hammer, the plot and the framework of the building will be bought up by another developer, who will complete the project with the expected product – a nice new house.

Sometimes the situation is different. For some reason, the customer decides to cancel the project and informs the team. The project management decides to bring the project to a close using their own resources, but with the help of an investor. A sponsor or other manager negotiates the rights to the product with the customer and finds the money. After the project is completed, the team receives the product and disposes of it according to the agreement with the investor and other stakeholders.

Early project closing is a special topic. Most experienced PM do not like this kind of result and try to draw out the work processes by all means, using any tools to avoid early closure. Whether this is worth doing or not is entirely up to the manager. An important guideline in deciding the issue will be whether it is appropriate to continue project work or to reach an early completion. Honesty and professional impartiality should be called upon to help. If you see that the product will not meet required quality parameters, why go out of your way to create the fiction of a successful case? Obviously, we all struggle to keep our reputations clean, but it's better to have pride and honestly admit your failures.

You may have noticed it yourself – if someone says that he has completed every project in his life in the most successful way, it is immediately clear that he exaggerates his merits. And if a person is able to distort the reality when looking into the eyes of an interlocutor, then it is better not to work with him – there is a clear sign of unreliability.

There is only one thing to add to what has been said in this sub-section: whichever option for closing the project you are faced with, analyze the course of events, get to the bottom of the reasons for the delayed closure and draw your own conclusions.

Intermediate Phase Completion and Project Closure

The project closure phase involves the same activities as the completion of each of the project phases, but at a much higher level. During project implementation, the manager conducts one by one the completion of all the phases, thereby preparing for the closure of the project as a whole.

By arriving at the closing, the PM already has all the intermediate completion acts in place, which allows him to simplify the project's final phase. By reviewing the paperwork for each phase, the manager recalls project development and draws conclusions about how effective and thoughtful the team was in achieving the goal. And given that he is in charge of the team, the manager also evaluates his own achievements.

Before announcing the end of the project, the manager also needs to compare actual results in terms of time, resources and workload with the plans made before the project started. The correspondence between set goals and how the planned activities actually took place can say a lot about the team and the project process.

Let's say the discrepancies are significant. So we need to find out how it was possible to get to the end in the first place? It turns out that the team was working in its own mode, ignoring the work schedule built around the plans. If this is the case, then it shall be acknowledged that the planning stage was extremely unsuccessful.

The above example shows how interesting and important the completion stage is! It is now that you see the whole project activity, from start to finish. You can work through the risks again, but in reverse projection, and see if you have calculated the most dangerous risks and if plans A and B have been effective. You can also easily see where the team performed better and where they lacked skills, resources or flexibility. It's all in the palm of your hand!

Don't miss an opportunity to reflect on what's happening and draw conclusions that will make next projects much more successful.

———eee———

Have All Works Been Completed?

Project or phase closure is the process of winding down all operations in each of the project management process groups to formally complete a project or phase. As discussed above, when closing a project, the manager reviews all previous information obtained during the completion of previous phases to ensure that all work on the project is complete and that the project has achieved its goals. Since the project scope is defined by the management plan, the manager analyses this document and compares target goals with actual results. If they coincide, the project is actually completed.

The closing process includes all of the actions necessary to administratively complete a project. They help achieve the following goals:

- perform the activities by which the team creates a product that satisfies project completion criteria;

- organize the actions by which the result (service or product) is sent to the next stage or customer acceptance if we mean project completion;

- and also collect the project documents or a phase, verify the success or failure, study the data obtained and save information for possible future projects.

A project can only be considered closed when these actions have been completed.

Feedback

It is impossible to summarise project activities if there is no feedback from stakeholders. At the end of the project, the project manager can organize it by developing a list of questions to which the customer, sponsor and other people who have overseen the project will provide their opinion.

The questions can be anything, depending on the project manager's area of interest. Often the PM will ask about the things that concern him or her most. He may have doubts about the quality of the equipment the team had to work with, perhaps he is concerned about project timing.

The questionnaire does not have to be voluminous and can sometimes be replaced by a heart-to-heart talk. Let there be just three discussion topics, but the most important ones. If a manager is interested in his colleagues' personal opinions on project implementation, he should add an extra line to his list of questions. The only thing is that it is no longer in his power to make him fill it in.

As part of obtaining feedback, the customer and sponsor can be invited to give feedback on the project team and the company that carried out the order, about the project manager personally.

Almost every PM considers it important to know what the team who worked with him thinks of the project. He or she can ask how the specialists assess the level of organization of the work, its pace, the provision of resources, and in response get an opinion on their performance. There is the option of conducting an anonymous survey, as team members are not always prepared to tell the truth.

If we are already talking about post-project work with the team, accept the recommendation to hold a debriefing meeting, inviting only your team members to it. Without the customer, managers and others. At the beginning of the meeting, give credit to each participant, try to talk about their contribution to the overall activity if possible, discuss the bad decisions and, in the end, reward the best ones. The next time you need a team, you will already have people you can rely on. They, in turn, will remember you as a leader they feel comfortable working with.

Conflicts sometimes arise during the project course and are not resolved until the project is closed. Figure out who is right and who is wrong, and fix the problem so that it does not happen again next time.

The ultimate pilot in interacting with your team is to help your former colleagues find new work on other projects if you are not planning to take on the next order now.

Management of Open Issues

The closing stage of a project involves dealing with open issues. An open question should not be seen as a conflict or dispute. We see it as just another problem to be solved specifically at this stage because it is the final one.

Let's say an open issue remains between the production department and suppliers. The manager should find out what the problem is and act as an arbitrator and mediator. Thanks to his control, the issue should be resolved.

If there is an open issue within the team, you need to bring together those on whom the decision depends, and work with them to resolve the problem. Sometimes it is not possible to resolve an issue on the first level, but it is necessary to involve the management or the people in the team who can find another way to resolve the disagreement.

Sometimes a special meeting is organized for this purpose, sometimes the issue can be resolved in absentia.

The open question and the way it is resolved should be recorded in the project archives and an administrator will keep a log.

At the end of the project, open questions create more problems and there is less and less time to resolve them. Nevertheless, project managers should not ignore them, because if problems accumulate but are not resolved, one day you will get a critical mass and an unplanned turn of events. If the open issue itself is not a conflict, then multi-day controversies are bound to breed one. It is also highly likely to have an impact on the budget, on interactions with contractors, on the timing of the project. As a result, much more serious measures will have to be taken that will require additional resources. How this will affect project implementation is hard to imagine, and there is no time to correct the situation – the project deadline is right around the corner!

—*ele*—

Project Closing Processes

When we speak of project closure, we mean termination of contractual obligations between the parties involved in the project at the moment when the customer accepts the product and signs the delivery-acceptance report. Now the project is considered completed, and the project manager is no longer responsible for the work on it (unless otherwise specified in the founding documents).

Closing the project, the manager must conduct preparatory actions: draw up the various documents, arrange the appropriate stage of activity, etc. Let's list the main ones.

Financial statements

When closing a project, the manager checks financial documents of his contractors, as well as the customer. It is necessary to check whether the current picture of calculations corresponds to the originally planned project budget. If the income and expenditures match, then the next step comes – certification.

Certification is the preparation of documents of a technical nature, which specify detailed information about the goods, and provides an extended description of their characteristics. The manager prepares quality certificates, equipment certificates, etc.

Let's specify that not all projects require it. For example, if the project product was a medicine, it is necessary to obtain documents that prove its safety and efficacy, but some services are not subject to licensing. Relevant documents are prepared in advance of the project handover stage, so there is usually no particular difficulty in dealing with this issue.

Reconciliation of Liabilities

In the course of project implementation, deferred liabilities arise, which have to be fulfilled before the project is closed in a mandatory manner. For example, some qualities of the product do not meet the customer's requirements – so the deadline has come to deal with this issue and create the very product that the customer will be happy to accept. At the same time, decisions are made to pay penalties if the obligation cannot be fulfilled. Usually, such situations are identified in the work of contractors, and you have to be prepared for this in advance.

Final Project Report

In this document, the project manager briefly and accurately describes the project's progress. He mentions the difficulties encountered, the problems, the solutions to these problems, the final description of all activities and the results obtained.

The final report is necessary both to give it to the customer and to understand the circumstances under which the project was implemented. This document encapsulates the manager's experience and becomes a prompt for the next similar project.

Warranty

Most products require a warranty period as they are items, things, computer programs that people will use for a long time. It is not the project team that takes care of the product warranty, but the manager has to organise this service and prepare relevant documents.

Final settlement

This is the document that really closes your relationship with the customer and stakeholders. The customer makes the final payment and you shake hands to say goodbye. Of course, this will be the case if he is satisfied with the team's performance, is happy with the product and has no complaints about it. Sometimes a perfect parting of ways is not possible, then penalties for defects or failure to deliver the product on time are discussed.

Among the tools and methods of project completion, it is recommended to use assessments by project experts or the opinion of specialists not related to the project but invited as independent consultants. They review the product, compare it with the customer's requirements and relevant quality standards accepted in this business area, and then conclude whether the project can be completed or whether improvements need to be made.

Acceptance and post project works

One of the most important acts of the project handover phase is the acceptance procedure.

During the acceptance process, the results of the project's final stage are agreed upon, and recorded in relevant documents. Once all details have been agreed upon, the PM proceeds with the product handover to the customer, then documents are checked, clarified and approved.

A set of documents shall be prepared for this stage, which includes:

- acceptance report,

- reports of remarks,

- reports of corrective actions;

- reports of the manager's meetings;

- report of the approval procedure.

The documents are prepared in duplicate, as one package stays with the customer and the second with the project manager.

By the way, some managers make a whole show out of accepting project results, inviting all project participants and even guests. If this idea seems acceptable, you should discuss it with the customer. If he or she is okay with it, and you are sure that the handover will be an entertaining show and everyone will be happy, then why not? According to the standard procedure, all stakeholders do not need to be present during the handover. The project manager, sponsor and team representative are enough. Sometimes there are individual questions for contractors, but these are taken up by the project manager and discussed with the contractors separately and at another time.

On the customer's side, the sponsor can sign documents, which does not contradict the rules of project management, but this is not always the case. The contract signed by the customer or sponsor means that the project is closed and the works are finished.

After project closure, an additional stage is possible – post-project work, which includes two main groups of activities:

- warranty service described earlier in this chapter,

- product user training, if necessary.

The project manager organizes a team of tutors or consultants with relevant skills and knowledge for training. Accordingly, a training plan, a venue for seminars or training sessions, and an opportunity to gain practical skills, i.e. to practise using the product, will be needed. The terms of training and results are agreed upon with the customer in advance.

The post-project work is useful not only for the customer but also for the manager, because he can evaluate his own work according to the criteria of warranty service. It may well be that the product is often broken, unstable when operating conditions change, or over time, reveals some defects that the developers did not implement before it worked in normal mode.

Such unpleasant facts sometimes teach the project manager a lot, it is his way through difficulties to the stars, and it should be taken with all possible patience. The profession of a project manager provides for constant improvement of the manager's skills.

As a result of project closure operations, the manager updates the assets of the organization's processes: entering data on the completed project into the project work archives. This list includes documents such as the project plan, cost calculations, work schedule and exact deadlines for each project phase, reports on change management and dealing with risks: which ones were envisioned, which of the backup plans worked and which did not, etc.

The project closure reports shall be saved. They include formal documentation with data about the completion of one stage and the beginning of the next.

—ell—

So, the project is initiated, launched, you have managed the team, customer expectations, risks, and other processes and activities during the implementation of your task. Now the project is complete and closed, congratulations.

But this is just the start. The project is closed and... long live the project!

1. The Five Dysfunctions of a Team by Patrick Lencioni

2. The New One Minute Manager by Ken Blanchard and Spencer Johnson

3. Radical Candor by Kim Scott

4. Herding Cats: A Primer for Programmers Who Lead Programmers

5. The Phoenix Project by Gene Kim

6. The Deadline by Tom DeMarco

7. Peopleware: Productive Projects and Teams by Tom DeMarco

8. Waltzing with Bears by Tom DeMarco

9. Mythical Man-Month by Frederick P. Brooks Jr.

Printed in Great Britain
by Amazon